Design for Growth

Design for Growth

Twelve Steps
for Adult Children

Veronica Ray

1817

A HARPER/HAZELDEN BOOK

Harper & Row Publishers, San Francisco

New York, Cambridge, Philadelphia, St. Louis
London, Singapore, Sydney, Tokyo

FIRST HARPER & ROW EDITION PUBLISHED IN 1989.

Library of Congress Cataloging-in-Publication Data

Ray, Veronica.
  Design for growth.

  "A Harper/Hazelden book."
  Bibliography: p.
  1. Adult children of alcoholics—Psychology.
2. Adult children of alcoholics—Religious
life. I. Title.
HV5132.R42 1989   362.2′92   88-45664
ISBN 0-06-255498-0 (pbk.)

89 90 91 92 93 BANTA 10 9 8 7 6 5 4 3 2 1

This book is lovingly dedicated to the next generation . . . with hope that knowledge and truth will set you free.

CONTENTS

ACKNOWLEDGMENTS

I acknowledge with deepest gratitude all the pioneers whose work in the field of adult children's issues and recovery helped to make this book possible. I also wish to thank Alcoholics Anonymous for the gift of the Twelve Steps; my editor at Hazelden Educational Materials, Rebecca Post, for her faith in me and in this project; my husband, my daughter, and my friend, Kathy A., for their unwavering support and encouragement; and the loving, healing, creative power of the universe.

INTRODUCTION

Yesterday we got what they gave us.
Today we get what we give ourselves.
Earnie Larsen

Twelve Step programs have helped millions of people recovering from chemical dependency and other dysfunctional behaviors. In this book each Step will be discussed. The specific focus will be on the problems of adult children of alcoholics and of other families with self-destructive behaviors. Nothing is new or strange about the ideas here. They're as old as philosophy itself and as classic as The Golden Rule. Most of us know them but may have feared trying to live by them. Some of us delude ourselves into believing that we are living by them and that our problems are caused by outside forces working against us.

But the rewards of working the Steps can be great. The program gives us a basis for getting and maintaining spiritual health and harmony. This program involves suggestions and helpful tools for healing. But whatever tools we use—Twelve Step groups, private counseling, friends, reading, writing, meditating—the healing comes from that place deep within each of us that connects us to our Higher Power.

These Twelve Steps were first written for Alcoholics Anonymous (A.A.). As adult children, we can adapt the Steps to our needs. In Step One, we can replace the word *alcohol* with the words *alcoholism, drug addiction, physical abuse, or sexual abuse.* This Step can also help us deal with how childhood experiences have affected our adult lives. In Step Twelve, we can replace the word *alcoholics* with *others* or *other adult children.* Our adaptation doesn't change the Steps. They can work as well for us as they have for millions of alcoholics.

This book will help to guide you through the Steps, to identify problems in your life, and to move toward healing. The Twelve Step program isn't a crash diet approach to recovery. We don't work the Twelve Steps in twelve days or weeks, and are then suddenly cured. We work each of the Steps fully, as gradually as we need to, at our own pace. Then we rework the Steps as we feel the need. We learn to live the Steps in all areas of our lives as we continue the lifelong process of recovery.

Those of us raised in families with alcoholism or other addictions may have thought that our troubles were over when we grew up and left our childhood homes. As adults, we may have wanted only to create new lives, to leave the past behind. On the outside, we may have appeared successful. But inside some of us continued to suffer deep anguish and uncontrollable, destructive behavior.

Our homes sheltered not only our families but also alcoholism, other addictions, and other problems such as physical or sexual abuse. This created environments of chaos, unpredictability, tension, and fear. As children growing up in such environments, we did the best we could to cope. We developed survival skills rather than living skills. We carried some of these behavior patterns into our adult lives. They may have sabotaged our growth and happiness.

We may recognize in ourselves some of the following adult child traits: low self-esteem, seeking approval, lying, mistrusting people, fearing anger and criticism, and feeling isolated. Other traits include feeling guilty and ashamed of ourselves, trying to rescue and be responsible for others, fearing abandonment, and becoming compulsive.

We may have convinced ourselves that other people or outside influences caused these feelings, attitudes, and behaviors. We might think our childhood homes have nothing to do with our adult problems. We may even deny and suppress our true feelings until we no longer seem to have feelings.

Eventually, we may realize that material comfort or success doesn't necessarily make us happy. We may keep behaving in self-destructive ways, but we can't seem to stop. It isn't essential to hit bottom before working the Twelve Steps. But most of us cling to old ways and familiar beliefs even when we're hurting. Only when some crisis or revelation occurs are we forced to see that something is terribly wrong and that we can't fix it alone.

We're now ready to accept the help we need: the Twelve Step program of recovery. It's a spiritual program, not a religious conversion. We need not have religious beliefs to use the Steps or to enjoy their benefits. The program works for people of all religious persuasions as well as agnostics and atheists. We need only be willing to view ourselves honestly, to try to work through the Steps, and to entertain the idea, however we choose to perceive it, of a Higher Power. Working through the Steps, we develop a sense of what our unique Higher Power means to us.

In this book, I use the words *God* and *Higher Power* interchangeably. They're meant to express whatever perception of this concept is meaningful to us. By surrendering our self-will to our Higher Power, we can release our emotional and physical suffering, and find new love, happiness, and growth.

If we open up our hearts and minds and let our Higher Power lead us through our recovery, the results will take care of themselves. Try to work the Steps, one day at a time, without expecting perfect results. All it takes is a commitment to work, to look honestly at ourselves and our lives, and to accept the help we need to heal. Day by day, we grow stronger and healthier. Our lives become less painful and complicated. Through our Higher Power, we learn to love ourselves and others, and find inner peace and serenity.

In the following chapters you'll see how various people have learned to identify their adult child problems and how the Twelve Steps have helped them to a better life. The names and examples used in this book aren't those of real people, but are composites based on the experiences of adult children. Any personal identification is purely coincidental, or the result of the common traits adult children share.

Now we can leave the path of mistrust, fear, and shame behind. We can begin the journey within.

STEP ONE

We admitted we were powerless over alcohol—that our lives had become unmanageable*

> *When will I learn to quit fighting lions?*
>
> — *Melodie Beattie*

Beginnings always seem hard, don't they? Change is scary. Right off in Step One, there's that word—*powerless.* Frightening, isn't it? Nobody wants to feel powerless. We try all of our lives to control situations and people. We like to think that we can create whatever we want in life and change whatever we don't want. But the family dysfunctions we've lived with have had their effects on us. We may find ourselves doing things that are self-destructive even after we think we know better. We may be just now recognizing our powerlessness over chemical dependency, other dysfunctions, and how their affects have made our lives unmanageable.

Can we manage our lives without help? Absolutely not. But we may have been taught from a young age to value and to use our brains and our egos to control and manage our lives. We may have believed that our bodies, talents, and intelligence could get us what we wanted. We may have tried to model ourselves after teachers, bosses, heads of state, and others who seemed to have the power to manage successfully. As adults, we may have not understood why

*Each Step quoted at the beginning of a chapter in this book is from the Twelve Steps of Al-Anon, adapted from the Twelve Steps of Alcoholics Anonymous, reprinted with permission of A.A. World Services, Inc., New York, N.Y.

the results from our actions never quite matched our expectations. Yet we may continue trying the same things that have never worked and never will.

Recognizing our powerlessness and the unmanageability of our lives goes against what many of us have been taught. It's a new way of looking at life. We may wonder how we can achieve our goals, believing we are powerless. We may argue that our lives aren't out of control—we've made significant achievements. Other people and events, we may believe, caused our setbacks. We may try every imaginable excuse to explain our problems rather than face our powerlessness.

The Truth about Power

Powerlessness is a terrifying concept—until we understand it, feel it, accept it. We may be afraid that admitting our powerlessness will cause our world to collapse. As children of chemically dependent or other dysfunctional families, we grew up in chaotic environments. To make sense of our world, to feel safe, we might have developed a deep desire to control everything and everyone in our lives. We've probably imagined that we could control others and fix our problems if only we were good enough or tried hard enough.

As adults, we may have wanted to create the false front of a controlled, stable life. To do so, we may have become obsessed with achievements or possessions. We may have rationalized our feelings of isolation, fear, and guilt. We may have blamed many outside factors for our self-defeating behaviors. We may have ignored our needs and pain for the sake of a facade. We may hold jobs, pay our bills, run a household, and raise children. We may have worked hard to build the appearance of an ordered, balanced, serene life. And yet, under close examination, we see that we were never really able to manage the things in life that are important to our happiness.

Believing that we had the power to manipulate people and events, we've only made ourselves miserable. In Step One, we're surrendering this mistaken belief. But we're not giving up power — we're accepting that we never had the power to begin with, and that we never will.

Relationships and events never turn out exactly as we plan. We often find that we persist in attitudes and behaviors that go against our better judgment. Many things, including our bodies, have been trying to tell us that something is wrong, but we have refused to listen. For most of us, it takes a crisis of such force that we can't keep up our self-delusions. We may find ourselves in a deep depression, an important relationship may end, or our health may get much worse. Whatever the crisis, it brings us a sense of hopelessness. For some of us, the sense of impending doom is enough to frighten us into looking at ourselves and our lives, and seeking help.

Laura's Story

"I know the exact moment it all came crashing down around me," Laura, an adult child, recalls. "We were visiting my husband's sister and her family. It was a 400-mile car trip, and I drove the entire way. I knew I couldn't stand sitting in the car while my husband drove. I knew I'd yell at him about his driving, and I was sure he'd get us lost. It was easier to drive myself.

"Anyway, when we got there, my sister-in-law put us in the living room on her sofa-bed. I saw an old mattress in the basement and wondered why she didn't put us down there—at least we'd have had some privacy. I was tired from driving and wanted to go to bed early, but they were all there, watching television. In the morning, I got up very early because I felt like we were in the way, right there in the living room. Besides, there was only one bathroom, so I took my shower and got dressed before anyone else was up.

"My sister-in-law didn't make breakfast until mid-morning, so I made myself a cup of tea and put the used tea bag on a saucer next to the sink. When she did get around to cooking, she threw out my tea bag. This happened over and over—I'd set aside a tea bag that had only been used once, and she'd throw it out. I couldn't understand how, on their income, she could be so wasteful."

Laura spent her visit trying to get everyone to have breakfast earlier and dinner later. She tried to give her sister-in-law cooking lessons and constantly spouted advice about everything from decorating to saving money. She went around tidying up, closing windows, and locking doors. Finding entertainment they all agreed on was impossible, so Laura sullenly went along with the others' decisions.

"We spent one day at the zoo. I had wanted to go to the beach, but no one else did. So we paid a ridiculous amount of money just to get into the zoo and spent one long, hot hour after another traipsing around looking at smelly animals. When we finally sat down for lunch, I couldn't believe what they were charging for a hot dog and fries, so I didn't eat anything. After that, we just kept walking and walking until I couldn't stand it anymore and insisted on going back to the house. I was tired and weak from not eating, and mad at everyone for making me spend the day at that boring, smelly zoo. I sulked all the way home."

When they got back, they were locked out of the house. There were two locks on the door, and upon leaving in the morning, Laura had turned a lock they apparently never used. No one had a key, and there was no other way to get into the house. Laura had locked all the windows to conserve on the air conditioning.

"I felt awful. I was hot, tired, hungry, and everyone was really mad at me. They had to call a locksmith to break the lock. It took over an hour and cost a fortune. My husband was furious and didn't even try to hide it in front of everyone else. We had a terrible argument.

"I knew, even as I was trying to defend myself, that I was wrong. I suddenly realized that I had to try to run everything. I just couldn't let them take care of things in their own way in their own house. I couldn't relax and go along with anything. Everything seemed wrong to me because it wasn't the way I would have done it. I'd had a miserable time and ruined everyone else's too. That's when I knew that there was really something wrong with the way I had been acting, and that I needed help."

Powerlessness

Just as Laura did, we arrive at Step One when we finally realize that our attempts to control and manipulate haven't worked. Our lives seem out of control. No matter what we do, things keep getting worse. We're forced to admit that something is wrong, and we can't fix it alone. Our lives have become reactions to the circumstances we have lived with as children.

In our secret thoughts, we may judge ourselves harshly. We may try to cover up our inferiority feelings by acting superior. We may even find ourselves attracted to people we can try to take responsibility for and rescue. Or we might remain loyal to people and relationships even when they make us unhappy. We stay loyal because of our deep fear of abandonment and our need for others' approval. Or we may find a stable, normal life boring or uncomfortable, and seek out drama and excitement. We may develop our own addictive or compulsive behaviors.

Most of all, we may deny the painful feelings from our childhoods. We may push them deep below the surface and lose our ability to feel or express them. This may cause us problems with intimate relationships, and we may find ourselves feeling blocked and depressed. This depression can make us unable to fulfill ourselves through our work or our relationships, or to enjoy life. We may even suffer headaches, anxiety attacks, stomach ulcers, or other ailments.

However our problem appears, it's an ever-present and progressive disorder. It may lead to a sense of hitting bottom — a painful and frightening crisis that makes us realize that our efforts to control don't work. We may suffer emotionally and even physically until we begin taking care of ourselves. That's why the First Step in the recovery process means giving up the delusion of control—of *power* over events and people. It's also admitting that the effects of alcoholism or other family dysfunctions are making our lives unmanageable. When we don't listen to our hearts, they cry and scream and rant and rave until, one way or another, they get our attention.

As we work the First Step, we can look at our lives and see clearly. Although we may have tried to change ourselves or to force people and events in our lives to be the way we want, we've never really been in control. Eventually, we realize that the power to change isn't found in our egos or personalities. We see that we can't do it alone.

Step One shatters the denial we've so diligently maintained. The alcoholism or abuse we've lived with has exerted its power over us, and we now face that truth. We admit defeat but not failure. There is no failure in not being able to accomplish the impossible. We had no control over our family circumstances. Even as adults, we can't control addictions and other family problems. When we realize this, we can learn to accept our powerlessness. And then we can get the help we need to recover from our childhood experiences and the effects those experiences have had on our lives.

Surrendering in Order to Grow

We're at this First Step toward recovery because, deep inside, we've felt our powerlessness and the unmanageability of our lives. Now we admit it to ourselves openly and accept it. We surrender our desire to run the world, because we know it isn't possible. Now we can begin to climb out of the depths of disillusionment, frustration, and despair. This honest look at ourselves prepares us for the work we can now do, Step by Step, in healing our lives. We're at the threshold of recovery.

Once we accept our powerlessness, we're free to live life more fully. We can relax, stepping back to look at where we've been. We soon feel the invisible hand of our Higher Power gently leading us in another direction. It's like being reborn—rediscovering that part of ourselves that's not ego, personality, or body. That tiny spark deep inside that has kept us alive through it all may soon grow to full flame. We can begin to move toward accepting success and happiness into our lives, knowing that we don't create or achieve them by attempting to control and manipulate.

Building a Strong Foundation

The road we now travel is not smooth or straight. It's a road that takes courage, commitment, and time to successfully travel. Step One calls upon our courage to be honest and confront our denial, and to accept our fears. It takes a commitment to recovery to take this necessary, if painful, First Step. We aren't judging ourselves; by honestly observing and accepting our denial and fears, we help improve our lives.

Time has been called a great healer. But we know now that we can't leave our problems to time alone and do nothing more about them. We can instead take the time we need to completely work through Step One and each of the Steps that follow.

Beginnings are hard. Change is scary. At this stage, we're like infants. We're learning a new way of living. Let's be gentle with ourselves now. We can allow our Higher Power to help us, to teach us, to lead us through the Steps of our growth and our healing.

In working through Step One, we build a strong foundation for our recovery. Accepting our powerlessness and the unmanageability of our lives will help us begin to overcome our negative past experiences. We can build upon this first, scary Step. Having acknowledged where we've been and where we are now, we can begin to move forward.

Now that we've seen and admitted our powerlessness and the unmanageability of our lives, where do we go? If we shouldn't try to control everything and everyone, what should we do? If we can't control our lives, who or what can? These questions lead us to the next Step on our journey.

STEP TWO

Came to believe that a power greater than ourselves could restore us to sanity

> *With hope in our lives, all else is possible.*
> — Amy E. Dean

Step Two has been called the Hope Step. After recognizing our powerlessness, we turn to a Power greater than ourselves that can give us hope. This Power can do for us what we couldn't do for ourselves. It helps us realize that positive change is possible, if we begin to look at ourselves, our lives, and the world around us differently. This hope can carry us through working all of the Steps fully, as we grow spiritually and change for the better.

Despite working Step One, we may still feel a sense of being stuck with the effects of our family circumstances, of being unable to do anything about them. Many things we've been doing and are attached to have been ineffective in dealing with our problems and should therefore be abandoned. We may feel sad and frightened at letting them go before we've replaced them with new behaviors.

Our sense of doom can now be replaced by faith in a Power greater than ourselves. It's a new beginning. We can now move toward accepting light and love into our lives, toward finding our spirituality. The old can give way to the new, bringing us toward true peace and serenity.

"Came to Believe . . ."

The first obstacle to working Step Two could be our closed-mindedness toward the existence of a Power greater than ourselves.

But many of us who are successfully working the Twelve Step program have been agnostics or atheists. We may have become disillusioned or even angry with our churches or religions. But, through working the Steps, we've opened our minds and allowed ourselves to gradually come to believe in our individual concept of a Power greater than ourselves. Some of us have found new meaning in our churches and religions; others of us have found a new sense of spirituality in nature or the universe. However our concept of a Power greater than ourselves evolves, it will be there for us throughout the Twelve Steps and for the rest of our lives. It will guide us and help us and heal us . . . if we let it.

We may have been raised in a religion in which an all-powerful, all-knowing male entity controlled everything and everyone. We may have questioned "His" keeping score of all of our "good" and "bad" deeds and thoughts. As children, we may have prayed and followed the rules taught to us in church. Still, we may not have found relief from our abusive homes. This may have led us to believe that God didn't exist or didn't think enough of us to respond to our prayers.

As adults, we may have learned to believe in scientific knowledge and proof. Some of us may have concluded that no evidence proves the existence of any Power greater than ourselves. Now we're being asked to come to an understanding of and a relationship with a Power greater than ourselves. It's fundamental to the Twelve Step program for each of us to develop a unique sense of spirituality.

It may help to look at the words we can use in describing a Power greater than ourselves. It's not necessary to use the word *God*. This word may remind us of our childhood religious training and trigger rebellion. Many people have found that by using other labels—such as The Universe, Cosmic Intelligence, The Light, Creative Energy, or Higher Power—they can avoid the negative reactions that certain words with religious overtones may cause. We may choose whatever words are comfortable for us. There are probably as many definitions of "a Power greater than ourselves" as there are people in the world.

In working Step Two, many of us find that it takes time to come to believe in a Power greater than ourselves, a Power that is capable of healing us. We can remember the A.A. slogan, "One day at a time," and allow ourselves to come to believe at our own pace. The important thing is to not automatically and stubbornly disbelieve, but to keep an open mind. Having an open mind is the beginning of the process of coming to believe.

". . . A Power Greater Than Ourselves . . ."

Some people in Twelve Step programs find it helpful to start by thinking of their Higher Power as the program itself, the Twelve Step group to which they belong, or the Twelve Step principles. Or the Higher Power can be an imaginary guide—a mother, father, friend, teacher—who can give us what our own parents could not. Whatever it is, we see it as a positive force — loving, understanding, and forgiving. It doesn't judge or punish. It will not control or condemn. It's there to help us, if we choose to accept its help.

In Step One, we admitted our powerlessness and the unmanageability of our lives. We came to understand that our self-will was keeping us from the healing we wanted. Now all we need is to be willing to open our minds to the idea that help is available through a Power greater than ourselves. Knowing that millions of others have been helped by the Twelve Step program is enough proof to help many of us come to believe. Those millions were people just like us: They felt disconnected from any sense of a Higher Power, their lives were out of control, and they were hurting. They came to believe and found success in the Twelve Step program. Wherever we're starting from, we can have the same success.

Bob's Story

Bob, an adult child, was raised in the Catholic faith and attended Catholic schools. He went to mass every day, served as an altar boy, and considered becoming a priest when he grew up. "I guess I stopped believing in God when I stopped believing in the Church," he recalls. "When I was a teenager, my mother went to our parish priest for marriage counseling. My father was an abusive drunk, and the priest told her 'that's just your cross to bear.' It was fifteen years before I again set foot in a church."

As an adult, Bob says he believed "God and religion were just fairy tales for kids, to keep them in line." When Bob finally did walk back into a church, he was severely depressed. "All I could think about was my misery; all I could see was bleakness. I was out walking one day, and I saw this big beautiful stone building with lots of stained glass windows and a banner that said 'Joy' in front. I wanted so much to feel that safe, wonderful feeling I'd had in church as a boy; so I went in. The place was empty, except for one man, who came over and started talking. I didn't know he was a priest because he was wearing regular clothes. I told him about my parents and how long it had been since I'd been inside a church. He said there was a difference between my relationship with the Church and my relationship with God. He said I was mad at the Church—at one priest, really—and that I had let that cut me off from my spirituality.

"He told me he had been in Vietnam and had seen greater faith spring forth and grow out there with no churches, no altars, no rosaries, and no priests, than he had ever seen before or since then. He said I was like one of those soldiers, with no support, with nothing around me but fields and trees and sky. He said if I wanted to be in the Church I'd have to listen to its teachings and follow its rules. But if I wanted a relationship with God, I should look within my own heart."

Although he now understands that even priests are human and make mistakes, Bob decided not to return to the Church. Bob's mother had sought help from someone who, at the time, couldn't provide it. Bob has accepted that. He has also accepted that this event has nothing to do with the existence of a Power greater than himself.

"I know that something made me go into that church, on that day, to talk with that priest," Bob says. "A Power greater than myself led me there, to let me know it existed and could help me. It really was a miracle."

It may help us to begin seeing the positive events in our lives as gifts from our Higher Power. A positive event can be anything from a chance meeting with a friend to finding a book with exactly the information we need. We may have been told once that some painful experience was "God's will" or was "just meant to be." Now we can turn that idea around and think of our wonderful, happy, and joyful experiences as God's will for us. Acknowledging the positive things that come our way helps us to see our Higher Power's presence in our day-to-day lives.

At first, we may need to simply thank the sky for the sun and moon, and the earth for our food. We can be grateful for our daily errands that bring us into contact with the community around us and the people who care about us. Maybe we ran into a person we enjoyed seeing, or saw a book that taught us something valuable. As this becomes a habit, we begin to see a force at work in our lives, giving us what we need, helping us along. This positive force is our Higher Power. Even before we believe fully, we can allow it to work in our lives and may begin to see the many ways it helps us.

". . . Could Restore Us to Sanity"

Another problem we may have with Step Two is the idea that we need to be restored to sanity. Here again, the problem is with words. It may upset us to think of ourselves, or our behavior, as insane. Most of us have thought of people as either sane or insane. We may believe people who are incapable of functioning in society are insane and should be locked up in institutions. The rest of us, we think, are sane.

But normal, sane people sometimes behave insanely in some areas of their lives. We now know we can no longer live the way we've been accustomed to. In Step One, we gave up our delusions of power and control. Now, let's define sanity as no longer attempting to do what we know is impossible, and learning to live without behaviors that are destructive to ourselves or others. This restoration of sanity is part of our journey that takes us to a place where we feel whole and at peace.

The Power greater than ourselves that we're coming to believe in can be a loving, positive force. It can help us turn away from negative behaviors and replace them with new, healthier ones. In our old way of living, we may have relied on no one but ourselves, because we trusted no one else. But trusting our self-will alone has led us to futile, destructive beliefs and behaviors. Knowing this makes us more willing to rely on a Power greater than ourselves to restore us to wholeness, health, and serenity.

Coming to believe is a process. It requires that we open our minds and become willing to have the blocks removed that are in the way of a relationship with a Power greater than ourselves. Each at our own pace, we come to believe and trust in the will of our Higher Power for us.

We've worked on open-mindedness in Steps One and Two. This has helped us accept that positive change can occur in our lives. One day at a time, we can begin letting our Higher Power work in our lives, gradually removing the blocks we've placed in the way. We're preparing a foundation of hope and faith throughout the Twelve Step program on which to build healthier, happier lives.

STEP THREE

Made a decision to turn our will and our lives over to the care of God *as we understood Him*

> *For each of us, there comes a time to let go.*
>
> — *Melodie Beattie*

Now it's time to take a leap into action—a leap of faith. It's time to let go of our controlling behaviors and allow our Higher Power to take over our lives. This is what's meant by the A.A. slogan, "Let go and let God." It's a phrase we can often remind ourselves of as we work through Step Three. The words *God* and *Him* are not intended to define a Power greater than ourselves for us. To paraphrase, Step Three says we're building a relationship with God, whatever we understand God to be. We use terms like *God* or *Higher Power* to refer to the Power greater than ourselves but not to describe it. We must each, alone, find our definition of and relationship with God.

Step One encouraged us to humbly and honestly look at our powerlessness. Step Two urged us to accept and believe in a Power greater than ourselves. Now Step Three teaches us to be willing to let go and let God take over our lives. This Step requires more than accepting the theory that God can take over our wills and our lives. It requires action. After working the first two Steps fully, we may now be ready to take Step Three, which takes us toward the peace and serenity that can be ours through our Higher Power.

We need to be sure we're really ready for Step Three. We ought to give ourselves the time to do the inner work needed to fully grow through each of the first two Steps. It isn't necessary, or even helpful, to rush. That's part of our old, controlling self-will. To surrender our wills and our lives to our Higher Power, we need to first accept our true powerlessness and come to believe in a Power that is greater than ourselves and capable of restoring us to sanity.

But it takes trust to turn over our wills and lives to our Higher Power's care. Thus, we need to understand God as positive, loving, forgiving, and acting always for our highest good. If we have a concept of a controlling, punishing God, we may fear what will happen if we surrender our will.

When we're ready, we let go of a small part of our self-will and ask God for guidance. It may be helpful to give up one specific problem at a time. We ask for help with our willingness to let go and to trust our Higher Power to handle the situation. For example, we may be in a relationship where we habitually worry and manipulate. We may have believed that we can make a person like us or accept us. We now consciously turn that relationship over to God and accept whatever happens. We may catch ourselves worrying about it or trying to make something happen. At those times, we can ask for help in remaining willing to surrender the relationship to God's care. Then we can ask God to handle the relationship in any way God chooses. The relationship may improve, deteriorate, or even end. Whatever happens, if it's our Higher Power's will and not the result of our manipulative behavior, we can assume that it's the best possible outcome. We can follow the same procedure for our work, our spouse's work, our home, our children, money, or anything else in our lives.

Susan's Story

Susan has had five jobs in four years. She always starts out full of enthusiasm and with high expectations. She really wants the jobs before being hired. "I'm great in interviews," she says. "I always think, *This job is going to be wonderful.* I hear all these great things about it, and I get very excited. I believe I've finally found the perfect job—or company—for me."

Her employers see Susan as bright, energetic, and cooperative. They're impressed by how quickly she learns tasks. But while Susan is learning the job, she's very impatient. "Every time I make a mistake or run across something I don't know how to do, I feel totally inadequate for the job. I'm afraid they're going to find out that they made a terrible mistake in hiring me and that I really can't do it."

During her training period, Susan works hard to make herself — and the job—meet her high expectations. Eventually, things start going awry. "As soon as I get to know my way around, I start noticing all kinds of things that are wrong with the company, the procedures, the people. I try to make or suggest changes, and I start running into brick walls. I start listening to other employees' complaints, and I get very upset about all the problems and injustices I see. The company and the people I work with start sliding down fast in my estimation. I get so disappointed and angry. I start hating the job, the company, the people. I hate getting up in the morning and going to work. This usually happens when I've been working some place around six months. I stop caring about my work and start looking for another job. Nine months is about tops for me to stay in one place. Then I find another job that I think is going to be wonderful, and it starts all over again."

To get off this destructive merry-go-round, Susan can turn her perfectionism and job problems over to her Higher Power. She can try to let go of her worrying and her controlling behaviors, and allow God to decide what's best in each situation. Once Susan has let go and asked her Higher Power to take over her work life, she'll learn to accept whatever happens.

Perhaps she'll learn she is in the wrong line of work and will find something better suited to her skills and talents. Or she may realize that she's capable and competent in her current field, and that she actually enjoys it when she has given up her unrealistic expectations. Those problems Susan used to worry about may not seem so important—or could even be resolved. By giving up her self-will and controlling behaviors, Susan can make room in her life for the will of God.

One Day at a Time

Another good way we can begin Step Three is to turn over completely one whole day to our Higher Power. For 24 hours, we can let go of our worrying and attempting to control anything or anyone. We can ask God to guide us through that day. We can check in frequently, asking our Higher Power to help us let go of our self-will and to act on God's will. We may soon discover that the world continues to spin quite well on its own, without our attempts to run everything.

At first, we may be tempted to analyze what our Higher Power is doing in our lives. We may think, *Was that a good thing to happen or decision to make? Do I agree with it? What would I have done differently?* It's natural for these thoughts to creep into our minds. But to truly turn ourselves over to our Higher Power's care, we'll need to stop second-guessing and come to trust in God's will for us. When we've surrendered our lives to God, we begin to accept whatever happens. We observe—we don't *judge*—the outcome of a day, or what happens to a problem we stopped worrying about. And we begin to see the miraculous effects of letting God take over.

Gradually, we expand this to all areas of our lives, all day, every day. In time, it becomes a habit. In the meantime, we keep reminding ourselves to let go and let God, and we keep asking our Higher Power for the help we need. We try to align ourselves with God's will and let it become our own. We let it happen; we don't try to force it to happen. It's like learning to swim. If we thrash about in the water, tense and fearful, we'll sink as surely as a stone. But if we completely relax and let go, the water will lift us up and we'll float. We can now relax into the flow of the river of life, trusting our Higher Power to take care of us.

This doesn't mean that we leap from tall buildings, convinced God will save us. We don't stop caring for our children when we stop trying to control and manipulate them. We don't go around spending money we don't have, expecting our Higher Power to handle the bills. In other words, we don't try to bend God's will to our own. What we're striving for is quite the opposite: we want to relax our ineffective human will and let our Higher Power's will guide us.

Because we don't always (or even often) know what's best for us, we ask for God to take over our lives. We ask to be shown what to do. We ask that our Higher Power's will, and not our own, be done. And we can be sure God will lead us into doing things that help ourselves or others.

Our Higher Power won't force itself into our lives. But it's available to each of us, anytime, if we ask for and are ready to receive its guidance. We still—and always shall—have a free will. But we have seen the destruction that self-will caused when we allowed it to rule our lives. In turning over our will to our Higher Power, we take the chance that God will take better care of us than we can alone. In time, we find that God does.

Choosing to let God's will become our own doesn't enslave us; it frees us from our human limitations. Ironically, the more dependent we allow ourselves to become on our Higher Power, the more independent we become. We're stronger when we combine our Higher Power's will with our actions.

Understanding God's Will

Step Three suggests that we turn over not only our problems but "our will and our lives" to the care of our Higher Power. This means turning over even those parts of our lives we thought we controlled successfully. God's care enriches every area of our lives.

Letting go and letting God will at first seem to give us more success and happiness than we ever thought possible. But working the Twelve Steps doesn't make our lives perfect, without pain or difficulty. What we're doing is learning how not to create problems for ourselves or increase our difficulties. We have caused ourselves failure and misery by ignoring and fighting our Higher Power's will.

Sometimes God's will is hard for us to understand. After we make a sincere decision to let go of our lives and wills, and ask our Higher Power to take them over, difficult things may still happen. We may not see their purpose right away. But if it's truly God's will, and not the result of our interference, there will be a reason. Perhaps the situation contains a nugget of truth we need to learn or helps us to meet someone who enhances our lives. Not getting something we think we want often means that getting it would have prevented us from getting something better.

Coincidences have made a difference in most of our lives. Perhaps in school we didn't make the football team or get a part in the school play. But if we had, we wouldn't have had time to join the school paper or yearbook staff, where we discovered our talent for writing or photography. That's an example of our Higher Power at work in our lives—presenting opportunities, not punishments.

When we spend a day constantly reminding ourselves to let go and let God take care of us and everything in our lives, we can learn about what happens and how we feel. If our car breaks down, instead of getting upset, we can ask our Higher Power to show us the purpose of this event, the lesson to be learned. Perhaps we need to slow down and see the true unimportance of whatever we were rushing to do. Perhaps we need to stop for a bit, breathe slowly, and think. Perhaps we need to notice the sunset instead of the rush hour traffic. Or perhaps the mechanic who helps us says something that changes us somehow.

Whatever happens, we want to try to flow with the day's occurrences instead of becoming angry or impatient. We will eventually see that it's our Higher Power at work and it's all for the best. We can ask God to help us remain willing to accept whatever comes our way, whether or not we immediately see God's purpose.

Accepting Whatever Comes Our Way

As we've seen, our Higher Power can take over our wills and work in our lives for our well-being, our highest good. Even if we don't understand what's happening, we can assume some unpleasant or confusing experiences are needed before better things unfold. Our Higher Power may lead us to stop taking care of someone whose life we're involved in. We can trust that the person is better off without our help. And we're better off spending our energies in other ways. Letting go means surrendering not just our self-will but also our controlling, manipulative behavior toward others. As adult children, we may have done much caretaking of other people. Our Higher Power may now lead us to care about those people without trying to control and rescue them.

Once we're committed to turning our lives over to God, we remind ourselves daily, if not more often, to let go and to accept whatever comes our way. Experience shows us that, when our Higher Power has taken over, everything has a purpose. As a result, we're led to exciting new things that help us grow. When we relax our control and surrender our will, God always gives us what we need, even if it's not what we think we want.

It isn't necessary to believe in this process completely at first. Just assume that it might work. When scientists or doctors look for a new cure or vaccine, they don't always know what's going to work before they experiment. They decide on a possible solution, assume it will work, try it, and then watch the results. Let's assume that if we truly believe that God can restore us to sanity, and if we have truly let go and turned over our will to our Higher Power, then even things that may appear to be negative are really for the best.

Throughout the process of turning our lives over to God, old fears will sometimes surface. When we become aware of them, we can ask our Higher Power to help us with them. Then we can surrender them to our Higher Power's care. We'll also sometimes fall back into our old destructive habits. We'll be tempted to interfere with our Higher Power's work. When this happens, we can observe our behavior and feelings and ask God for help to move forward.

Perfectionism is a trait common to adult children, and we must try not to let it hinder our working the Twelve Steps. Not one of us is perfect and we know that our Higher Power is loving and forgiving. God, as we understand Him, will never lose patience with us and will always be there for us.

Recovery is not a contest. It's a healing process. We're giving up that inner tyrant who says we must control and succeed at everything. Surrendering our lives to our Higher Power's care means accepting our limitations and learning to depend on God to help us transcend them.

Building Our Foundation

When we've truly worked the first three Steps—admitting our powerlessness, believing in a Higher Power that is capable of restoring us to sanity, and turning our wills and our lives over to that Higher Power—our lives are already better than they have been, or than we thought they could be. We've stopped trying to manage our lives. But others may think that we are, for the first time, managing them beautifully. Our Higher Power is managing things for us. We're allowing ourselves to become vehicles for God's love and positive, creative energy.

The relief and peace we've begun to feel isn't the end of our road, but rather a good, solid beginning. We have built our foundation. If we've worked carefully and completely through these first three Steps, our lives are in our Higher Power's care, and we're ready to move even closer to true peace and serenity.

STEP FOUR

Made a searching and fearless moral inventory of ourselves

*Our willingness to face the negative
also reveals our true merits, essential
goodness, and numerous options—
possibly for the first time.*
— *Earnie Larsen*

Taking this inventory is an important Step on our journey. It can help us to see ourselves and our lives honestly and clearly for the first time. It can help cause many old, repressed feelings to rise to the surface and be released. It can help us begin a lifelong habit of careful reflection and honest observation, enabling us to maintain the peace and serenity we are now working toward. With God's help and guidance, we take a moral inventory, identifying our strengths and weaknesses and make progress toward recovery.

By now, we've learned that the Twelve Step program involves much self-examination. We've accepted our powerlessness, confronted our spiritual deficiency, and surrendered our wills and our lives to a Higher Power's care. With God's help and our newfound objectivity, we're now ready to examine our lives in specific detail. We search ourselves for character traits, both positive and negative. We search our lives for behaviors resulting from those character traits and look at how those behaviors affect our lives. We make objective, nonjudgmental observations, taking care to not slip into our old patterns of denial.

Denial is our insidious enemy throughout our Twelve Step program. It's a deeply ingrained habit in adult children. Many of us have used it to survive our childhood environments, to avoid a deep emotional awareness of things we couldn't possibly control, and to deflect responsibility for making positive change. We've used it to cover fear, anger, and feelings of worthlessness. It has served us well and hurt us deeply. If we don't surrender it now and watch closely for its reappearance, it will hinder our progress in recovery.

With honesty and humility, we can now draw up a balance sheet of our moral strengths and weaknesses. This will help us remind ourselves of our strengths, our positive traits. We can now recognize these strengths as our Higher Power's help or will at work in our lives. It will also remind us of our weaknesses or defects, and the resulting behaviors that hurt ourselves or others. We take this inventory in the present, searching for traits we now have and recent examples of behavior caused by these traits. This helps us to make a thorough and fearless inventory of ourselves and our lives.

Fearlessness may only be possible once we've come to humility and acceptance of our Higher Power in our lives. As long as we denied our problems and were obsessed with controlling, manipulative behaviors, we couldn't look honestly at ourselves and our lives. Without acknowledging our Higher Power's forgiving love, we couldn't face reality. Now that we've surrendered our self-will, though, we can trust God to take over any obstacles in our way. With our Higher Power guiding us, there's nothing to fear.

The Written Word's Power

In our inventory, we not only list our character traits and behaviors. We also record our perceptions—the beliefs, ideas, and attitudes that form the basis for our actions. Regardless of their relation to objective reality (or lack of it), our perceptions are what we act on. As adult children, our perceptions are often clouded by fears and resentment. These can be thought of as faulty perceptions based on unhealthy experiences. As we make our inventory, we can remember to turn over these resentments and fears to our Higher Power, asking for help with honesty, humility, and thoroughness.

We can write down our inventory lists on paper. The written word has power that transcends thoughts and spoken words. When we write something, we're giving it a tangible form. It becomes real to us. This helps us overcome our deep and pervasive denial. We've become expert at fooling ourselves in our minds. And we often deny spoken words, telling ourselves or others, "That's not what I meant," or "That's not really what happened." But once we've written a thorough, honest inventory of ourselves and our lives, we can look back over it, accept it, own it, and use it as a tool in our healing process. It can reveal truths to us that we have not been able to see.

Carl's Story

"I thought I knew exactly what would happen when I took my first personal inventory," says Carl, an adult child from an abusive background. "I was used to constantly bashing myself for every little thing. I'd lie awake in bed at night thinking of all the ways I had screwed up that day. Accusing, blaming, and hating myself for who I was and everything I did was just the way I lived."

Carl learned to treat himself this way as a child in a punitive, violent home. But taking his Fourth Step inventory was a very different experience than he had expected.

"I thought taking an inventory just meant writing down all those things I hated about myself. I went about it very methodically. I divided my life into different areas—work, family, friends, et cetera. I wrote pages and pages of what I thought were terrible things I had done and faults that were part of who I was — all the things I had agonized over night after night.

"Reading over my inventory, a pattern became clear to me. Was accidentally breaking the copy machine at work a negative behavior or character defect? Of course not. No one even blamed me for it except me. Was forgetting something on the grocery list or not being home when a friend dropped by a flaw or weakness? In every area of my life, things like that showed up. I had written dozens of things that had nothing to do with destructive behaviors. These were things that I thought made me a terrible person."

Carl used that inventory to help him work on another one that focused on the real problems in his life, starting with low self-esteem. "Writing it all out made many things so clear to me for the first time. I began to realize that those little mistakes and accidents weren't destructive, but the way I felt about them was. The inventory process helped me focus on the real problems, and I stopped wasting time and energy beating myself up for being human."

Looking at Our Lives

Like Carl, many of us who grew up in dysfunctional families tend to be very hard on ourselves. An honest, realistic inventory can help straighten out our perspective. We can stop denying our true defects and at the same time recognize the harsh and inaccurate judgments we've made on ourselves. We can then move on to dealing with the real issues in our lives and free ourselves of imaginary ones.

In the following pages, character traits shared by adult children will be discussed. Examples of each trait will also be given. Write down each trait that applies to you. Write about how each trait shows up in your life. Give specific, recent examples of each, citing the persons involved, where and when the incidents took place, and what you did and said. Be as thorough and accurate as possible. Remember that this is an exercise in self-discovery. Take the time you need to work through this inventory completely and honestly. Be aware of tendencies to deny the problems. Observe, don't judge. And remember that your Higher Power is available for help and guidance whenever you need it.

Isolation

We may have often felt that ou childhood homes were little islands, separate from the rest of the world. Whatever went on there was secret. We learned not to risk having over friends from school or socializing too much. We learned not to let others get too close to us or know us too well. We created a lonely prison within ourselves, certain that exposure would cause rejection and pain.

As adults, we often continue this isolation. We're unable to break the pattern of keeping people at a distance. We compartmentalize our lives, careful not to let our working relationships become personal relationships, or our neighbors become our friends. We may have become comfortable with this, calling ourselves homebodies or loners. And yet, we feel disconnected from the rest of the world.

This painful separation from other people may be a result of our unhealthy pasts.

The reasons we may fear inviting people into our lives may be located deep in our unconscious minds. Giving a simple dinner party may create so much anxiety in us that we decide it's not worth the bother. We may turn down invitations or even not show up at all when we're expected because of the same anxiety or because we're afraid of having to reciprocate. We may find ourselves sabotaging every possible new friendship.

We can now list ways we've acted out this inner isolation in our lives. Our list can include specific examples of recent behavior showing when, where, and how we've isolated ourselves from others. It can also include the people involved and our relationships to them. Then we can write down what we believe are the underlying feelings that led to our behavior. We should remember not to judge but to observe.

We may feel embarrassed or foolish about writing, "I believe nobody could like me if they ever got to know me." But feelings and perceptions aren't always rational and logical. Even if we know what we're feeling is unwarranted, we can accept that we do feel it.

Fear of People and Authority Figures

This trait is similar to isolation but involves more than just keeping to ourselves. We may have grown to distrust people, particularly authority figures. As children in dysfunctional families, we may have had authority figures in our homes who were insensitive to our needs and feelings. They may have also been unreliable, often angry, and even cruel. We learned as children that our place in the world was unimportant; nothing we did was good enough to make our parents or others in our lives happy. We may have grown to be automatically fearful of and intimidated by authority figures.

As adults, we may show this fear by being hypersensitive to anyone whom we view as having power. We may compare ourselves to others and feel inadequate. We may take aggressive, abusive behavior from others and not stand up for ourselves. Or we may mistake others' assertiveness as attacks against us.

Underneath our behavior may be a deep perception of ourselves as weak, inadequate, undeserving, and worthless. Listing these kinds of behaviors, we can again notice the difference between what we think and how we feel. We may tell ourselves on a rational, logical level that people have no particular interest in hurting us, and yet we may react to the slightest criticism with deep depression, anxiety, or rebellious anger. We may tell ourselves that authority figures are people who perhaps have more knowledge or experience than we have, and they are trying to do their best, the same as us. Nevertheless, our old unconscious reactions may be triggered simply by their positions of authority.

We can now list specific, recent examples of this trait shown in our work, our dealings with doctors, lawyers, ministers, government employees, police, bankers, and others. People in positions of authority need not only be our bosses. Many times we may be intimidated by and overly sensitive to strangers we deal with such as waiters or plumbers. We may feel guilty, anxious, and submissive because we see them as superior. We may accept haircuts we don't like, poorly prepared food, and outrageous bills. We may even blame ourselves for our clogged drains or faulty pipes.

These feelings are unnecessary and unhealthy. We can see them for what they are by looking closely at the resulting behaviors. We see who is involved, when and where we show this fear, and what we do and say. Do we feel depressed and worthless when someone in "power" doesn't shower us with affection and compliments? Do we assume that in a disagreement we must have been wrong and the other person right? Does minor criticism bring out feelings of failure and inadequacy? Listing specific incidents can help us to see the reality behind our perceptions.

Approval-Seeking

As children in a dysfunctional environment, we may have never received unconditional love and approval from our families. Consequently, as adults we may express no personal needs or opinions that might risk others' disapproval. We may lie, pretend, or suppress and deny our feelings. We may come to depend on others for our opinions and decisions and do anything to please.

One reason for our behavior may be we don't know who we are. If we've acted in ways we believed would win us the approval we so badly wanted, we've probably ignored things we need for health and well-being. We may have tried to find happiness through others. By giving others whatever we think they want, we believe we will get love and approval back. When that doesn't happen, we blame ourselves, and try even harder to please. We often continue this pattern in a relationship for many years. Despite not getting anything positive from a relationship, we may remain steadfastly loyal. In doing this, we are seeking validation for our very existence from others.

We can list the people we are involved with in this kind of relationship. We can list recent, specific examples of approval-seeking and denying our needs and feelings. What specific things do we do believing that they will make someone like us? What are we afraid will happen if we stop our people-pleasing behaviors? How have we enmeshed ourselves in this way of living? Do we have trouble refusing any request? How do we think others would react if we said no? Becoming aware of specific behaviors in this area helps us to grow less dependent on others' approval and more conscious of our feelings, needs, and opinions.

Caretaking

As children, we often were caretakers for our families. We looked after our parents, kept them out of trouble, hid their alcoholism, and soothed their pain. We may have acted as a parent for our brothers and sisters, watched them, helped with homework, drove them to ball games or school. We cooked, cleaned, pampered, protected, and mediated. These behaviors stunted our growth as we developed an insatiable need to be needed.

Caretaking is like approval-seeking, except that instead of giving others whatever they want, we give them what we think they need. We take responsibility for them, trying to rescue them or solve their problems. We make ourselves indispensable to them. This behavior, though, helps us keep denying and avoiding our problems. We lose ourselves in relationships with people who we take care of, and we neglect our needs. We become long-suffering martyrs to others who we think depend on us.

As we list our caretaking behaviors, we may discover that people don't really need much of our help. We may be stopping them from finding their own way, discovering their own connection to a Higher Power, and living their own lives. We're also avoiding our problems and developmental tasks. It's easy to slip into denial and convince ourselves that these people desperately need us. Perhaps we've found another addicted person to take care of just as we took care of our parents (or saw one of our parents take care of the other). Perhaps we compulsively devote ourselves to our children, unaware that we are really keeping them from developing their identities, strengths, and self-esteem. Perhaps we believe, deep down, that others won't like us or want us around if they don't need us. Our inventory can show us how, by adopting everyone else's problems, we've been avoiding our own.

Frozen Feelings and Repressed Anger

As adult children, we often have a hard time expressing emotions. In childhood, we learned to cover up our feelings because they made us vulnerable in our family circumstances, or because we saw so many inappropriate and frightening outbursts of uncontrolled emotions in our homes. Whatever went on in our homes may have had to be kept secret from others; we may have not talked about it even within the home and family. Our feelings were kept just as secret. We learned to suppress these overwhelming feelings. We may have decided that no emotions could be safely felt and expressed. We denied our feelings and developed a deeply ingrained habit of suppression.

As adults, we may be unaware of our unexpressed emotions, not realizing their connection to our depression, resentment, and even physical illnesses. We may have become emotionally numb, with a kind of dead zone inside us, preventing feelings from being registered or expressed. But unexpressed feelings don't go away. They go deep inside us, creating stress, anxiety, and illnesses.

The habit of suppressing feelings can also create problems in adulthood with intimacy and other kinds of relationships. Our numbing response may be so automatic that we honestly don't know how we feel at any time or in any situation. We may have even cut off our ability to recognize and express our good feelings along with the scary, negative ones. Having lost touch with our emotions, we may believe we feel nothing.

In listing our behaviors, we may have to look hard at every situation and relationship to discover the feelings we're automatically stuffing deep inside. At first, we might list our nonresponses to people, events, and circumstances. We can record whatever we discover, not judging but merely observing. Perhaps after visiting a friend, we arrived home with a terrible headache or some other physical symptom. That's a clue to repressed emotions. Perhaps we're angry or resentful toward someone, or life in general, and don't know why. Perhaps our anger and resentment is more general, underlying many of our interactions with others.

Adult children often hold much suppressed anger inside. As children, our anger toward our parents and others may have frightened us, and we denied and suppressed it. As adults, the suppressed anger may feel sometimes like a ticking time bomb inside us. It may cause serious resentment and depression. It may create painful physical ailments and stress-related illnesses. Repressed anger doesn't just go away. It becomes a part of us until we bring it into the light and deal with it.

In making our lists of suppressed feelings, the underlying emotions themselves may be harder to get at. We can begin by watching our physical and mental health, and our inappropriate or distorted responses. We should keep close watch for our resentments and jealousies, and our unexplained grief and depression. Beneath these lie old, repressed emotions.

Control

In our childhood homes, little was under control. Nothing was under our control, as we were only children. Life was unpredictable.

We lived often in tension and fear, at the mercy of our family problems. As adults, we may have reacted to this childhood experience by adopting the opposite extreme. We may have tried to control everything and everyone. We may have tried to control our emotions and behavior, and others' impressions of us.

As children, we couldn't always rely on others, so as adults, we may refuse to even try. We may strive to be not only self-sufficient but in command of events and other people. We can become obsessed with control, certain that letting go will cause the kind of chaos and confusion we suffered in childhood.

This underlying fear may show itself in our overreaction to change. We may be demanding of the people in our lives or too rigid to take advantage of unexpected opportunity. We may be intolerant of others' opinions, new ideas, or new ways of doing things. We may become anxious in situations where we feel loss of control. This rigidity and need for control may make it hard for us to trust others or to relax and have fun. We may not be able to enjoy unstructured time or unplanned pleasure.

In our inventory, we can list recent, specific examples of manipulative, controlling behavior. Have we interfered with the natural course of a relationship or situation? How have we reacted to unexpected events? How have we responded to new thoughts or ideas from other people or to people who didn't agree with us? Have we trusted others to live their lives, or have we manipulated them and the events in their lives? Have we felt compelled to tell people what they should do, even when our opinion was not asked for? Have we become backseat drivers in other people's lives as well as in their cars? How have we felt and behaved when people didn't behave as we wanted? By listing specific examples of our inflexibility, we can begin seeing our underlying desire for complete control.

Low Self-Esteem

This trait is common among adult children. It can permeate every part of our lives and affect everything we do. Many of the behaviors we've already discovered in working through Step Four result from this character trait. In our childhood homes, we may not have received the dependable affection and care needed to grow up sure of our self-worth and identity. Because we were often surrounded by adults whose self-esteem was very low, we may have never developed a key ingredient of a healthy, happy adulthood—a true sense of self.

Low self-esteem hides behind many behavioral masks. It may show in our excessive dependency, perfectionism, and even cold, superior attitudes toward others. Or it might show in our lack of assertiveness, feelings of inadequacy, and negative self-image. It may have even led to self-defeating compulsive behaviors such as overeating.

As we write down our behavior caused by low self-esteem, we may find our lists overlapping. Low self-esteem may cause approval-seeking or caretaking behavior. Isolation and fear of other people may come from low self-esteem. Other symptoms of low self-esteem may include over-responsibility, unhealthy sexual behavior, and fear of being abandoned. We may be unable to recognize and enjoy our accomplishments. We may believe that nothing we do, think, say, or want is valuable or deserving of the same respect we give to others. Listing specific recent examples of these kinds of behaviors can help us to see, hidden beneath them, the low self-esteem.

A Searching and Fearless Inventory

These examples described on the previous pages are the most commonly identified character traits of adult children; they give us a guideline, a place to begin. When we take a personal inventory and think about these traits, we may uncover other traits equally troublesome. Many people in Twelve Step programs use the Seven Deadly Sins—pride, greed, lust, dishonesty, gluttony, envy, and laziness—to inventory their problem behaviors. But the method we use in making our inventory isn't important. What is important is that we make a searching and fearless inventory. We need to write down specific examples of the negative character traits we'll try to let go of in our recovery process.

If we've completed the first three Steps fully and made a searching and fearless inventory of ourselves, we may now have the clearest view ever of our lives. What we've written can be an invaluable tool for growth and recovery. We've discovered ourselves. We've uncovered ourselves. We've painted a picture of our weaknesses and strengths. Having fully taken the first three Steps, we may have already begun to change old behavior patterns. The inventory is of recent behavior, and present attitudes, beliefs, and traits. We've probably discovered some previously unknown strengths. We've probably also found a few spots where we could say, *I've always done that, but yesterday, I did this.* Once we turn our lives over to God, we may notice some changes for the better. Let's remember now to accept everything we've found without judgment, to surrender to our Higher Power, and to ask for help to proceed. What we've done thus far will never be lost if we use it, learn from it, and let it transform us. We can move on from here and return whenever we need to. It is ours.

STEP FIVE

Admitted to God, to ourselves, and to another human being the exact nature of our wrongs

> *The secrets we keep, keep us from the health we deserve.*
> *Each Day a New Beginning*

In Step Four, we examined ourselves for character defects that have led to our faulty perceptions and self-defeating behaviors. If we've made a balanced inventory of our strengths and weaknesses, we've also found positive traits and behaviors that encourage healthy self-esteem. We have more of a complete picture of ourselves and a realistic view of our lives. If we have been honest and thorough, our inventory can now become the tool to use in taking Step Five.

In Step One, we talked about the courage and commitment and time needed to work through the Twelve Step program. Step Five requires a great deal of courage. But we now have a foundation from which to draw strength. The work we've done thus far and our relationship with a loving, understanding, and forgiving Higher Power can give us the courage to proceed. Our commitment to this healing process can also come from our Higher Power and from our concern and respect for ourselves and others. If we've taken the time needed to work the first Steps fully, we've discovered the value of letting ourselves grow through the Steps rather than trying to force or fake change. We can come to think of time as an ally on our journey of self-discovery and recovery.

Having given our inventory the power of the written word, we can now take our self-examination even further to the power of open, honest disclosure to our Higher Power, ourselves, and a person we trust will understand. We can now admit to ourselves the exact nature of our self-defeating behaviors. By now we've developed faith in our loving, forgiving Higher Power—or we have at least begun to act that way. Our Higher Power's love and forgiveness can help us to forgive ourselves. In taking this Step and talking to our Higher Power about our faults and mistakes, we can find a new sense of trust and love. Many people in Twelve Step programs have felt their first real, deep connection to their Higher Power in taking Step Five.

We now accept our place in the human community by facing another person without our old defenses, delusions, and denial. We can now accept our responsibility by sharing our true selves with another person. Our behavior—which evolves from our character traits, beliefs, and attitudes—affects others and the whole human community. We now accept this responsibility and admit our self-defeating behaviors and negative character traits as they relate to others as well as ourselves.

Being Candid with Others

The value of talking to another person about ourselves is also well-respected by psychiatrists and psychologists. "Talk therapy" is often part of treatment for depression, anxiety, and many other disorders. It's a healthy, helpful exercise. It gives us an emotionally safe environment for expressing feelings long kept secret. It also gives us another person's point of view to shape a healthy, realistic perspective on ourselves and our lives.

When we share ourselves with another person, we see ourselves in a new way. This can help us release our old patterns and move toward healthier relationships with ourselves and those in our lives. This Step can be hard for those of us who are unaccustomed to being open about ourselves with other people. Honesty and openness imply being truthful, forthright, candid, and sincere in an unobstructed flow going both ways. We give information to the other person and, at the same time, grow more aware. Talking with another person about our character flaws with honesty, humility, and trust can begin to shatter our isolation, denial, and delusions of control and self-sufficiency.

For many adult children, trusting another person may be a new experience. We may have believed that others would reject us if they knew the truth about us. We may worry about dumping our problems on other people. But do others only want to see a facade of glory and perfection? Remember, it's our character defects we're now facing and admitting to them may make us fearful. The reality is that people are often far more understanding and loving than we thought possible. When we reveal ourselves to one another—all of our weaknesses and imperfections—we become closer.

Janet's Story

The secrets of Janet's abusive childhood home kept her from revealing herself or her feelings to others. She lived isolated from other people. "When I was growing up, I couldn't tell anyone about the drug abuse and incest in my family. But it was so much a part of my life that the only way I felt safe was by not saying anything. I had no friends because I never got into the long phone calls and slumber parties where the girls got together and talked on and on about everything: their families and things they did together, boys, dreams of the future, romance, sex, whatever. They thought I was just real shy—or stuck-up. I felt like a locked case, a Pandora's box of emotions and memories."

As an adult, Janet moved away from her family. But she remained reticent and isolated. Like many adult children, she never shared much of her self with others. She kept a cool distance between herself and the rest of humanity. "I had friends, but I never really opened up to anyone. I never talked about myself or my feelings or anything like that. When people asked me how I was, I always said, 'fine,' no matter how miserable I felt. I thought I had to keep up a certain image for other people. And it didn't include any weaknesses or problems.

"Admitting my flaws and negative behaviors to myself was easy. I was always analyzing my behavior because I was so afraid of becoming like the rest of my family. I tried hard to understand where

I had come from and how it had affected me as an adult. But I never talked about it with anyone. I was terrified of revealing so much of myself to another person."

Not talking became a deeply ingrained habit in Janet. It kept her isolated for many years. When she finally did share herself with another person, it was scary. "It took me months to find someone I trusted enough to talk to about myself. I chose a therapist, because I thought her professional standing and ethics would make her trustworthy. I wasn't even sure what I'd gain. But I went ahead and did it anyway. It felt strange at first. But as I talked, I realized that the sky wasn't going to fall on my head because I had opened my mouth. It even started to feel good.

"My therapist seemed to understand and accept what I said. She asked questions and pointed out things I hadn't thought about before. I felt so cleansed, so free and light, as if a great weight had been lifted from me. All I had done was talk and put some truths out where they could be heard by someone else. It also helped to see them myself, more clearly than ever before. I never would have believed that talking to another person could make me feel so much better."

Purposeful Self-Disclosure

Like Janet, instead of trying to make our fears go away, we can move through them—taking Step Five in spite of them. Remember, the object here is to reveal ourselves, to accept the realities of our lives—not to blame, explain, or defend, and not necessarily to obtain forgiveness from another person. Whether or not people forgive us is up to them. It's up to us to completely and honestly admit our defects.

Our talk with another person isn't an exercise in gossip or self-pity. It's purposeful self-disclosure. Our purpose is to claim our secrets and at last unveil our true selves. Our motive is a commitment to recovery.

Some of the anxiety we feel may be relieved by selecting the right person to talk to. This person should be someone we can trust not to betray our confidence, someone who can provide honest feedback without being judgmental. This person can be a doctor, minister, counselor, or friend. Or this person can be a stranger—perhaps someone in a Twelve Step fellowship. It should be someone who can understand, listen, and offer helpful feedback in the form of questions or comments. We may even find it appropriate to share some things with one person and other things with someone else.

When we've chosen someone with whom we feel comfortable, we should explain our mission so the person knows what we're trying to do. We should set aside time, in a place free of interruptions. There, we can be candid and thorough and allow the other person to respond. We should remember to accept whatever feedback the person offers and not to slip into defending ourselves.

We don't have to talk about future changes here. We're admitting our past behavior and current character flaws that cause self-defeating behavior. Having another person to talk to in this way keeps us honest. It finally breaks down our denial system. The shock and shame of our deep secrets, once revealed, is diminished. When we shine light on even the deepest shadows, they disappear.

Sharing ourselves with another person in this way can make us feel a new sense of ourselves as people, not so very much different from others as we had thought. We feel, perhaps for the first time, the acceptance of another person even with our true selves revealed. Our self-worth increases, and we feel a new kinship with humanity. We've shared our burden of guilt with our Higher Power and with another person, and found understanding and acceptance. We've seen and openly admitted the truth about ourselves. The relief we now feel can be nourishing and strengthening.

When we've admitted our weaknesses to God, to ourselves, and to another person, we can begin to move forward with a new grasp on the truth. We can now truly see and accept ourselves. We have not suddenly become perfect. But we've become a little better and moved closer to peace and serenity. We've gained some sense of self-worth, perspective, and relief from our fears.

We may still continue old, ingrained habits and lapse into destructive behaviors. Instead of hating ourselves for our weaknesses, we can now accept ourselves and remember that this is a healing process. We're learning and growing constantly. Looking for an overnight cure was part of our old controlling behavior. We now want to focus on each Step as we take it, mindful of our ongoing recovery. Every day we are someplace in our lives that we need to look at closely and experience fully. The journey is the destination.

STEP SIX

Were entirely ready to have God remove all these defects of character

Readiness is the key to all important passages in life.
— *Earnie Larsen*

We've now examined our character defects and found traits that produce negative behaviors. We've admitted to God, ourselves, and another person our behaviors and the underlying character traits causing them. Yet we may still be continuing behavior harmful to ourselves or others. We may still try to control things or isolate ourselves from others. We may still suffer from the disabling low self-esteem we developed as children of dysfunctional families. We can turn to our Higher Power who can remove our character defects. But first we must be ready.

Why don't we just go ahead and ask God to remove our defects, without wasting time worrying about our readiness? Being "entirely ready" means believing that our Higher Power can and will remove our character defects, if we ask humbly. It also means being willing to accept what we ask for.

While we may be ready to have some of our defects removed, we might have deep attachments with other defects. We may not be so willing to have God remove our desire to attempt to control things. We may not be ready to give up our self-will, our dishonesty, or our dependency on others. We may think we're ready to have all of our character defects removed, but aren't ready to have our lives changed by it. We have grown accustomed to our defects and may not be ready for change.

We've developed some defects as tools to survive in a dysfunctional environment. We may be very reluctant to give up these traits because of deep unconscious fears of not being able to live without them. We may cling to old familiar patterns because what is new and different frightens us. Or we may be afraid that God will remove something we like from our characters. Are we really ready for change? Are we really ready to let our Higher Power decide what kinds of changes will take place? Do we really want to have our character defects removed and are we truly ready to accept their removal?

We have, through these Steps, developed a relationship with our Higher Power. We've begun to trust in that Higher Power. But we may still be afraid to let go of our self-will which we may still think will bring us success and happiness. We may still think that through our willpower, we can eliminate our defects and get on the right track. We may be having a very hard time letting go. We may fear that God will change us and our lives in ways we don't want changed. We may fear what will be chosen for us, if we let go.

These fears come from not having fully worked through the previous Steps. Have we truly admitted our powerlessness, turned our will over to our Higher Power, and thoroughly examined and admitted our character defects? The fears may also come from old negative tapes we play in our minds about good and bad, right and wrong. We may fear that to become "good" we will have to give up our pleasures in life. The old tapes that were drummed into us in our homes, churches, schools, and by society may tell us sex, pleasure, success, and happiness are bad, beauty and art are frivolous and worthless (or even evil), and suffering and pain are good. We may be convinced our Higher Power is equivalent to the old tapes, and if we allow our Higher Power to remove whatever it chooses from our characters, our lives will become dull and unpleasant or even more painful than before.

Giving Up Our Defects

Once again, we can give up our negative tapes when we begin to trust that our Higher Power's will is for our highest good. We may find that things we've never been able to enjoy, our Higher Power wants us to do joyfully and without guilt. As for those things our Higher Power doesn't want us to do, we will stop wanting to do them when we have truly accepted God's will for us and become ready to have our defects removed. We can let our Higher Power remove our defects and see what we have left.

We can take the chance that our Higher Power loves us and wants only the best for us. Our Higher Power can lead us to greater success and happiness than we ever dreamed possible. But first we need to let go of our self-will and accept that our Higher Power knows better than we do what will bring us happiness and success.

We may fear giving up our defects because we don't know what our lives will be like without them. We might fear we'll live lives of austere self-sacrifice or boring inactivity. Presuming that God will lead us to this kind of unhappiness is defective thinking. We know by now we've been wrong about many things. God will remove only that which is destructive in us and leave us with what is constructive and uplifting.

In Step Two, we came to believe in our Higher Power's ability to restore us to sanity. We defined insanity as character traits and resulting behaviors destructive to ourselves or others. We may have grown attached to some of our character defects. But if God is to restore us to sanity, all traits and behaviors that are ultimately destructive will have to be removed. With more trust in and experience with our Higher Power, we learn that some things we believed to be destructive weren't. And other things, which we believed weren't destructive, were. Working through Step Six helps us let God decide what's to be removed from our storehouse of traits and behaviors, and what's to be left behind for our betterment.

Remember, the Twelve Step program doesn't try to tell us what's right and wrong, or good and bad. It guides us through thoughts and actions that help us to discover ourselves and our connection to a

Higher Power capable of bringing our lives to happiness and health. It's a spiritual program, not a moral one. *Spirituality* can be defined as our relationship with our Higher Power. Morality, which is a specific code of moral rules and conduct, has nothing to do with the Twelve Step program. If we let go of all we have absorbed as children of dysfunctional families and let our Higher Power guide our thoughts and actions, chances are we'll do nothing destructive toward ourselves or others.

Becoming the New You

We know now that we cannot, by ourselves, remove our character defects. The only thing we do in working Step Six is to allow our Higher Power to work in our lives. We examine our attachments to our defects, face our fears about having the defects removed, and let go and let God. Millions of people who have worked the Twelve Steps enjoy full, satisfying, joyous lives. They haven't sacrificed anything positive. This fact can help us to let go and trust God to do the same for us. When we let our Higher Power remove our character defects, we open ourselves up to even greater joy than we ever thought possible. Without our defective character traits, we can have full and happy lives.

Becoming ready to have our Higher Power remove our character defects takes time. As we've worked these Steps, we've gradually become ready to have our defects removed. We're now asking God to remove some of them. We may have done much of this unconsciously. What we are aware of is change—relief from some of our old, destructive behavior patterns.

Now we're ready to make a conscious effort to let go of the more stubborn, deeply rooted character traits that cause our destructive behavior. We may need to ask for God's help to attain the willingness and acceptance to accomplish this.

Jonathan's Story

After college, Jonathan moved away from his family to his girlfriend's hometown. Her family appeared to Jonathan to be the kind of large, close-knit group he had dreamed of as a child neglected by his parents. He was determined to become a part of it, to belong. He set out to win over every family member, adopting their ways and agreeing with everything they said. He showered them with gifts and favors. The only problem, as Jonathan saw it, was Tom, his girlfriend's brother. Tom was close to his age and held the position in the family Jonathan wanted so badly.

Jonathan became very competitive with Tom, trying to outdo him in everything from sports to income to kindness. "Everything Tom did, I had to do better," Jonathan recalls. "I just had to get into that family, and the only way I could see to do that was to take his place. Every time anyone said anything positive about him, I saw it as a threat to my position in the family. If Tom bought new clothes, I bought more expensive ones, even though I couldn't afford them. If Tom talked about a new restaurant or dry cleaners or shoe store he liked, I had to find a better one. If he gave his girlfriend a sweater, I gave his sister diamond earrings."

Jonathan's competitiveness with Tom expressed itself in many ways and lasted for many years. In his marriage to Tom's sister, Jonathan began working on his adult child issues, but he remained very competitive with Tom. It became a sore point in his marriage.

"I always said I couldn't stop competing with Tom, but my wife said I just didn't want to. I thought she was really unfair and insensitive. Eventually, though, I realized that she was right. I didn't want to stop. There was a payoff in it for me — feeling that I was okay, that I had a secure place in my wife's family as long as I was better than Tom. I didn't want to give that up for anything."

Gradually, Jonathan learned that feeling good about himself had to come from within, not through outside achievements, and certainly not at another's expense.

"I feel better about myself now than I did when I was trying so hard to feel good about myself. The attachment I had to competing with Tom was hurting me when I thought it was helping me. Letting go wasn't easy. But now I don't feel like the good feelings I have can be taken away from me. I know those feelings come from the Higher Power working inside me."

Relinquishing Our Self-Will

Communicating with our Higher Power has been an increasingly important part of our lives as we work these Steps. By accepting our Higher Power's will, we've begun to see how it works in our lives. We may have also heard our Higher Power's voice within us. But this is difficult unless we quiet the noise of our conscious thoughts, rationalizations, and old "should" tapes.

Our Higher Power speaks to us, not always in words, but through our inner voice or intuition. We may have once had a deep sense of inner truth. But as children, we received messages and pressures from outside ourselves: *Don't be disrespectful toward your parents. Don't make the family look bad to outsiders. Don't talk about the problem. There is no problem.* Our families, schools, and even churches have influenced us to disconnect with this inner voice of truth. We may have suppressed and distrusted our intuition, and, like Jonathan, looked for approval from other people.

Our relationship with our Higher Power may have been ignored, suppressed, or even replaced by relationships with people, churches, schools, and jobs. These outside forces may have filled our minds with ideas about how we should think, feel, and behave. Is it any wonder that, as adults, we sometimes have difficulty hearing our Higher Power's voice clearly, or knowing which of the many voices in our head is our Higher Power's?

We hear the voice of our intuition—our unconscious center, our heart, our Higher Power—when we relax our hold on those other voices. We let go of all those tapes and rationalizations inside our heads and ease the power we've given to those other voices coming from outside our spiritual centers. We learn to recognize the voice of our ego, amid all the others, and to relax its power over us.

When we become ready to give up our character defects and to trust that our Higher Power will remove them, we are choosing to become free—free from our old weaknesses and the delusive voices in our heads. We'll have no more excuses for destructive behavior and that may scare us. But our faith in our Higher Power is increasing through these Steps, and we find our trust growing while our fears diminish. Readiness comes through working the Steps day by day, faithfully. As we grow in faith, we gradually stop getting in God's way. We can ask our Higher Power for help in seeing and admitting our defects, in letting them go, and in trusting God to remove them.

By doing so, we're choosing the path to freedom. We're becoming liberated from our character defects and free to let our Higher Power heal us and choose for us. We're becoming free to move forward in our recovery and get even closer to peace and serenity. In return, we're giving up nothing of real value. Becoming ready to have our Higher Power remove all of our defects brings us closer to God's infinite love and our ultimate well-being.

STEP SEVEN

Humbly asked Him to remove our shortcomings

> *Tackling with God's help that which seems impossible, reduces it to manageable size.*
> *Each Day a New Beginning*

We're now ready to ask God to remove our character defects and have them removed. Or are we? In Step Six, we thought we prepared ourselves by accepting that our Higher Power could and would remove our defects. We also became willing to accept whatever result might occur from God's removal of our defects. But at the very core of Step Seven there's something we've been working on right from the start in Step One—humility. The need for humility underlies the entire Twelve Step process and is at the core of Step Seven. It isn't something we concentrate on in one Step and forget about in the next Step. It's basic to our recovery from dysfunctional upbringings.

Humility doesn't mean beating ourselves up for being human. It means accepting that we are human and imperfect. Sixteenth century Dutch scholar, Erasmus, wrote, "Humility is truth." Truth is what we've sought from the beginning of these Twelve Steps—the truth of our powerlessness, our defects as well as our strengths, and the help available to us through our Higher Power. Humility helps us to see the truth, the realities of ourselves and our lives. It enables us to accept ourselves as we are: good but not perfect; trying our best but not always succeeding; and with our Higher Power's help, able to find peace and serenity.

Our humility began when we gave up our battle with alcoholism or other family dysfunctions and turned it over to our Higher Power. Becoming humble, accepting humility as the cornerstone of our recovery, means accepting the reality of our powerlessness. It's bringing God's healing and loving power into our lives. As children, we may have tried to become self-sufficient because we could find no one to trust. Learning to trust God takes time and constant working and reworking of the Steps. Working through the first six Steps has helped us to begin to see ourselves, and everything else, differently. We can now ask our Higher Power to remove our self-defeating behaviors and accept our Higher Power's healing love with humility.

Barbara's Story

Like many adult children, Barbara learned to take care of herself at an early age. "There wasn't anyone there for me. Whether I was sick or hungry or tired or needed help with my homework, no one was there. I felt like I lived alone while my alcoholic parents tried to run a small business. By the time I was in junior high, I cooked, cleaned, and shopped for myself. And I walked or took the bus everywhere I needed to go. In high school, I did all that plus I helped run my parents' business, collected on debts, and paid the bills. My motto in life was, 'If you want to get anything done, do it yourself.' "

As a young adult, Barbara was proud of her independence and self-sufficiency. She viewed people her age as frivolous and imma-ture. "All they ever wanted to do was have a good time—partying, spending money foolishly, and shirking their responsibilities and obligations."

Barbara's conscientiousness brought her great success as a college student and a worker. Although she sometimes felt tired and over-whelmed, she never accepted help. A friend going to the laundro-mat, offering to do Barbara's laundry, was refused even though Barbara could have used the free time. A co-worker's offer to give her a ride to work while her car was being repaired was likewise rebuffed. When Barbara was sick, she went to school and work anyway, refus-ing offers of class notes or help with shopping or errands. "I really hated being sick. I used to think that if I ignored every cold or flu I got, refused to give in to it, I could will it away. I thought I could do everything on my own. I didn't want to feel dependent on or indebted to anyone. I believed that I didn't need anybody, and that's the way I liked it."

When doing an errand one Saturday morning, Barbara was hurt in an automobile accident. "My injuries weren't terrible," she recalls. "None of the damage was permanent or anything. But it was bad enough to keep me in the hospital for a while. My leg was in a cast up to my hip, and I had trouble getting around. I had to ring for a nurse just to go to the bathroom. I was a miserable patient, blasting anyone who came to see me—doctors, nurses, and friends. Most of the time, I laid in bed and cried about all the things I couldn't do for myself.

"Gradually, I saw that I had no choice but to accept my situation. I had to let someone go to my apartment to water my plants, feed my cat, and pick up my mail. I started letting the hospital volunteers bring me books and magazines from the library. I let a physical therapist teach me how to use crutches and a wheelchair. For the first time in my life, I realized that I couldn't do everything for myself. I started to relax, to trust, to let other people do what they could do for me."

Barbara's physical recovery was slow. When she went home from the hospital, she still needed help with things like laundry, shopping, and transportation. She took disability leave from her job, even though not working made her uncomfortable at first. Work had been her way of life since childhood. Accepting the help she needed from others was not easy for Barbara, but she learned how and lived better as a result.

"Learning to accept help taught me that I never really have to be alone. I have all kinds of resources that I didn't have as a child. I can't do everything myself, and I don't have to try. Help is available. Alone, I got by, I survived. But now I really appreciate having other people in my life. I have better friends than I ever knew and lots of other people who can help me. Everything is much easier and much more fun."

Barbara learned that accepting the help she needed enhanced her life, rather than making her weak or dependent. In the same way, we can now accept our Higher Power's help in removing our self-defeating behaviors and traits.

Reviewing the Steps

Asking our Higher Power to remove our defects and then having them disappear may sound too easy. Perhaps we aren't ready to believe that it can work. Or maybe we still want to rush through the Steps, wondering what the big deal is about each "little" Step. Step Seven is where we realize how much work we've done and how much we still need to do. If we ask God to remove our character defects and nothing seems to happen, it may mean we need to review the previous Steps. We may need to work at becoming truly humble and ready to have our character defects removed.

In working Step Seven, we continue believing in our Higher Power and trusting that we will be relieved of our weaknesses when we've done the necessary work. We ask God again and again to take over our wills and our lives. We review our inventories, examining them for honesty and thoroughness. We notice any changes in us and our lives since beginning this journey and remember to thank our Higher Power for our progress. We ask for help with willingness to do the necessary work and to accept changes. We consciously stop our controlling behaviors that interfere with God's work in our lives. We humbly ask our Higher Power over and over again to remove the character defects we, by ourselves, cannot will away.

Saying The Serenity Prayer at least once a day reminds us to let God make the choices of what can be changed and what can't.

God grant me the serenity
To accept the things I cannot change,
The courage to change the things I can,
And the wisdom to know the difference.

If we believe that God can restore us to sanity, we'll let it be done. Instead of presuming that we can do everything ourselves, we can now let our Higher Power choose what's best for us.

Other reasons exist for our defects not being removed immediately upon asking. One is the possibility of wheels being set in motion of which we are unaware. We may need time to see and feel the changes within us. We may think, impatiently, that we don't feel any different. Our impatience is a symptom of our old, defective thinking. We can ask our Higher Power for patience and remind ourselves again that working the Steps is a healing process, not an overnight cure. As we work to break down our old barriers, as we work and rework the first Steps, as we accept God's ability to remove our defects, we also accept God's way of doing it—however long it takes and however it changes our lives.

Our defects themselves can also impede their removal. The low self-esteem many adult children feel can create guilt in asking for anything, from anyone, anytime. We may feel, deep down, we don't deserve to be healed. We may modify requests to our Higher Power with ideas like, *I know you have a lot more important things to worry about. . . . I know I should just accept the lot in life you've given me.* We may feel particularly guilty when other family members still suffer but refuse to seek help. We may compare our adult lives to our childhood and feel fortunate. We should be happy with what we have; *it could be much worse,* we may rationalize.

Here again, we need to recognize the old, negative tapes playing in our heads. If we understand where they are coming from, and that they are part of our problem, we can minimize their power over us and proceed without their interference. By humbly asking God to remove our defects, we acknowledge our powerlessness to remove them by ourselves. Humility is truth, not guilt based on low self-esteem. Humility helps us recognize God's power. Guilt as an outgrowth of low self-esteem—more appropriately called shame—is a defective character trait and an impediment to our healing process.

Our Higher Power Can Help

Confusion might be another reason we may not see the immediate removal of our defects. Even after making a sincere Fourth Step inventory, we may not have fully understood our strengths and weaknesses. If, for example, we've asked God to remove our desire for power, but it's not taken from us, perhaps our problem isn't with ambition. Maybe it's with our greed and disregard for others.

On the other hand, our Higher Power might find it necessary to remove character traits that we may never have thought of as defects. We may not notice when they're gone. Most of us don't consider giving up a character defect unless it's clearly and directly causing us great pain.

Many people find it easiest to focus their prayers on one defect at a time. Using our inventory, we can rank defects we still have from the easiest to give up to the hardest. We can then ask our Higher Power, specifically and often, to remove the easiest one. When we feel relief from that one, we remember to thank God. Then we move on to the next one, and so on.

Remember, we aren't doing the removing ourselves on a conscious, ego level. We're letting our Higher Power do it for us. We're staying out of God's way. When we've completed this process, we thank our Higher Power and ask for any remaining defects to be removed even if we are unaware of them and don't know enough to ask for their removal.

As we proceed through the removal of our weaknesses, we may catch ourselves occasionally falling into perfectionism, a common adult child trait. The goal of Step Seven—and the entire Twelve Step program—isn't perfection. It's self-improvement: going from a confused, painful life to a peaceful, loving life, guided by a benevolent Higher Power.

We may have, while working the Steps and in the rest of our lives, moments of great clarity, peace, deep love, and happiness. We also have times of confusion, fear, and doubt, when we wonder whether we've made any progress. We should realize that we never become perfect, any more than a child suddenly becomes completely mature or educated at eighteen. Life is a process. We grow through the Twelve Steps, learning positive ways to work through the process and with the process.

Letting go of our character defects and allowing our Higher Power to remove them may leave us with a temporary sense of loss. Change, even welcome change, can be unsettling. Giving up defective parts of ourselves can be like having restorative surgery after a disfiguring accident: The new skin may be more beautiful and healthy than the scar tissue. But our new face takes some getting used to. We can adjust to the changes by remembering that God has only removed that which prevented us from living full, happy, healthy lives.

Room to Grow

We may find that the removal of our character defects is met with some resistance by others. Persons who have become used to our approval-seeking or caretaking behaviors, for example, may resent the changes in us. They aren't used to us being honest or refusing to do things they expect. Others may resent us when we no longer join them in destructive behaviors or unhealthy relationships. Some people may be upset, thinking we're not acting like ourselves. They may like to pigeon-hole people and know exactly what to expect from them at all times. These people may be losing something they aren't ready to give up, and are being challenged to change and grow themselves.

We should remember that change is scary and difficult for others just as it is for us. Our main obligation is to our own recovery. We don't set out to hurt anyone, nor do we enjoy others' negative reactions to our growth. But it's up to them to deal with the effects our positive changes have on them. Realizing we must each grow in our own way and time may be helpful. Before we asked our Higher Power to remove our defects, we became willing to accept whatever happened as a result, including changed or ended relationships. We don't need to feel guilty about these relationships even if others are angry at first. Truly positive changes in us can only have positive results.

When we've sincerely asked God to remove our shortcomings and accepted whatever has happened in our lives as a result, then we can trust that our Higher Power wants us to have and improve the strengths we are left with. We can begin, with our Higher Power's help, a lifelong process of weakening our weaknesses and strengthening our strengths. Strength in all people grows from practice, from exercise.

We can begin giving our strengths a real workout now, unimpeded by our old defects that have been removed.

With our wills and our lives in our Higher Power's care, we no longer have to worry about wrong decisions regarding strengths and how they can be improved. God gives us intuition about what to do, and we can learn to hear and trust our intuition. We can grow in strength and wisdom every day of our lives. We can remember to give God credit for our positive changes, and to be continually thankful.

Improving Our Outlook

Low self-esteem may make us unwilling or unable to follow things through, to finish what we start. This makes it all the more important to constantly attend to our ongoing recovery process. We can work the Twelve Steps every day in praying, meditating, observing our behavior, noticing change, reading, thinking, talking, listening, and writing. We can also let go of our self-will again and again, develop our relationship with our Higher Power, and accept God's will for our lives. We must follow through and keep at it always.

We can watch our tendencies and behaviors and ask for our Higher Power's help in continuing to weaken our weaknesses and strengthen our strengths. We can keep on improving, learning, and growing if we regularly recite and put into practice the words of The Serenity Prayer.

STEP EIGHT

Made a list of all persons we had harmed, and became willing to make amends to them all

> *The state of a relationship's health is dependent upon the state of health of the people involved in the relationship.*
> — *Amy E. Dean*

The first task in this Step may appear fairly simple. We make a list of all the people who have been harmed by our character defects. Now that we've taken a personal inventory, it should be easy to list the persons we have harmed, right? It may not be that simple.

Again, as in Step Seven, humility is the key to a successful Eighth Step. Humility is truth. Our defective traits and behaviors may have hurt others, even though we may have had good intentions. Some behaviors we learned as children helped us survive and grow up despite our dysfunctional families. We needed them. Now, as adults, we need to recognize their negative effects on our relationships and let them go. We don't uncover the truth to punish ourselves, but to clear the way for new, more positive behaviors and relationships.

First we need to examine our life histories. Our Step Four inventories can help us identify people we may have harmed recently. We also need to look back over long-forgotten events and relationships. We have, through these Steps, improved ourselves and given up some of our defective traits and behaviors. But that doesn't undo past damage. As we list every person by name and each specific event where we caused someone physical, mental, emotional, or spiritual damage, we may encounter some denial and resistance to uncovering these offenses. We may come up with excuses and distorted memories to avoid confronting the effects we've had on others. Step Eight, like each of the other Twelve Steps, is needed to move us forward toward peace and serenity. We can't, however, move forward while the past still weighs us down.

As adult children, we've been injured by others' defects and behavior. But nursing our resentments and grudges can only obstruct our recovery. Letting go of old resentments is helpful, even necessary, to finding sanity and serenity.

If we examine our past relationships honestly and completely, we can surely find faults in others. But in working Step Eight, we focus our attention only on our part in every harmful incident, understanding that we are not more perfect than others.

In examining our past relationships, we strive for objectivity, favoring neither side but recognizing our behavior that has been damaging to another person or persons. It's only by using this realistic view of events and relationships, and remembering that we are all imperfect, that we can forgive ourselves and others and begin to move forward in our relationships.

Let's define harm as physical, mental, emotional, or spiritual damage. As we examine our motives and actions, we can see how we may have harmed others. We may discover some cases where a person didn't seem to be harmed, although our behavior toward them was clearly destructive. Perhaps we lied to them or gossiped about them, and they never found out. That doesn't mean they weren't harmed. It's also possible that people sometimes haven't let us see how they were harmed. Our negative actions also may have harmed ourselves. As we search through our past histories, concentrating on our own behaviors, we can gain an honest view of the effects our actions have had on others.

Developing New Survival Skills

As adult children, we tend to have certain traits and behaviors that affect our relationships. For example, our deep-seated denial may have caused us to react angrily to someone trying to show us another, perhaps more realistic, point of view. Denial also causes lying, both to ourselves and others. Denial and suppressing emotions may cause us physical suffering. They also may bring our spouses, lovers, children, and friends emotional suffering from being cut off from someone they love. We learned denial in our childhood homes. But we continued using it as adults, convincing ourselves that those childhood experiences haven't affected our adult behavior. We've learned and admitted, through these Steps, that such beliefs weren't accurate or honest. But we may still want to deny that anyone else has been harmed besides ourselves.

We often suffer depression and physical ailments from suppressing our emotions and denying our problems. These illnesses may greatly affect others in our lives. We may have neglected caring for our children. Or we may have missed work often or been ineffective on the job due to repeated illnesses. We may have lost a job, creating financial hardship for our families. We may have created an erratic and unhealthy example for our children and others who depended on us for support and guidance. We may not have been there for others when they needed us.

Regardless of what our behaviors have been, we must remember that they grew out of the survival skills we learned as children in dysfunctional homes. We can extend the same understanding to ourselves as we do to others, and forgive ourselves for carrying these habits into our adult lives. We must remember we were only children when we experienced the negative circumstances of our family lives; we did the best we could. As adults, we're now ready to give up these old habits. Clearing our conscience of the negative effects these habits may have had on others can help us to move forward into a new, healthier way of life.

The need for control we may have developed in an uncontrollable childhood environment may have affected many people in our adult lives. At work, school, or home, we may have been difficult to work with on projects requiring team effort. We may have sabotaged loving relationships by not allowing ourselves to feel vulnerable. We may have stifled our children's development and self-expression by trying to control every aspect of their lives. Or we may have bullied others with unwelcome advice. Remember, our desire for control grew out of the needs of the child we once were. As we admit the negative effects this has had on others in our adult lives, we can forgive and understand ourselves.

Helping Others by Helping Ourselves

Caretaking is another kind of controlling behavior. Perhaps we've assumed so many of other people's responsibilities that we've enabled them to wallow in their helplessness. Perhaps we've enabled friends or loved ones to remain addicts by denying that they have a problem and covering for them. Perhaps we've sabotaged our children's growth by removing every experience, decision, and responsibility they might learn from, even through error or failure.

The lives of people we care for aren't harmed but enhanced by our caring. People we take care of, though, are hurt when we obstruct their growth and development. Caretaking may have fulfilled some of our defective needs; we may have believed we were helping someone else. But this kind of self-serving help hurts us both. We're now learning the difference between positive caring and negative caretaking. We can help ourselves move toward more positive relationships by admitting how our caretaking behaviors have affected others.

Approval-seeking behaviors can result in pretending with and lying to others and ourselves. Rather than sharing ourselves with others, we may have played approval-seeking roles. Lying hurts everyone and lowers trust in each other. Our need for approval may also have led us to do many harmful things because, as approval seekers, we had a hard time saying "no."

Approval-seeking may have led us to spend money foolishly, while trying to buy friendship or love. We may have agreed to fulfill obligations we were in no position to fulfill. We may have broken promises because we couldn't refuse a request or admit our limits. In our attempts to please everybody else, we may have neglected obligations to people who rightfully depended on us. We know now that constantly trying to please everybody is impossible. Seeing clearly how such behavior hurts us can help us improve our relationships with ourselves and others.

Our low self-esteem can also harm others in our lives. We may have behaved arrogantly or rudely toward strangers and loved ones to cover up feelings of worthlessness. We may have indulged in promiscuity or betrayed a faithful lover because of our insatiable need for ego-boosting. We may have become excessively dependent on a friend, lover, or family member (even a child) because our lack of self-esteem kept us from venturing out into life on our own. This dependency may have made that person feel responsible for us, impeding their growth in life.

We may have become perfectionistic, putting down every effort of ours or anyone else's as never good enough. This can be particularly harmful to our children or other loved ones who try to please us in various ways. Turning over these behaviors to our Higher Power may have already created wonderful changes in us and our relationships with others. Understanding our effects on people and relationships can help us to avoid slips and backslides in these areas.

Improving Our Relationships

Low self-esteem may also have caused us to fear abandonment. This can damage loving relationships if our behavior is possessive to the point of being stifling. It may also have led us to compulsive behaviors such as smoking, overeating, and other addictions harmful to ourselves and others in our lives. Our low self-esteem and sense of shame may have led us to lie about our backgrounds and ourselves. It may have made us incapable of pursuing a vocation or developing our talents. This behavior denies our potential contributions to society and harms our families, employers, and ourselves. Recognizing these past events can help us look forward with a better understanding of our place in the world and the contributions we can make.

Our isolation from other people may have often led us into harmful behavior. We may have refused invitations and overtures of friendship, causing others to feel rejected and denying them the connectedness they need to feel with others. We may have distanced ourselves from even our friends and families. Step Eight is about examining our relationships. None of us is an island. We can now accept how we may have hurt other people and move on toward more healthy, happy relationships.

There are countless ways we may have harmed others: lying, cheating, ingratitude, anger, criticism, rudeness, gossip, sexual infidelity, or selfishness. By avoiding recovery from our character defects, we may have harmed our friends, our loved ones, and ourselves. When we harm another person, one or more of our defective character traits is involved. We can identify these as we list the people we've harmed and how we've harmed them.

Our traits and behaviors affect more people, more deeply, than we may have realized. They affect friends, acquaintances, co-workers and business associates, lovers, neighbors, parents, children, spouses, and other relatives. They also harm us. When we've carefully listed individuals and how we've harmed them, along with the ways we've harmed ourselves, we can begin to understand our place in the world and our responsibilities toward all people. We can see ourselves and the effects of our actions more clearly and avoid repeating past errors. We need to do this to relieve our old guilt feelings—to clean out the old business so we can move on to leading new, healthier lives.

Penny's Story

Penny was a middle child in a family of five children. She learned early in life that the key to getting attention from her alcoholic father was her attractiveness. Her brothers and sisters were either smart, athletic, or lost in the family shuffle. Penny was pretty, sweet, and charming, especially when her father was around. She spent much time and energy on her clothes and hair, always dressing up for her father. By being his beautiful little girl, she was assured of his attention and affection.

Throughout her adolescence and adulthood, Penny won over men by using her appearance and behaving sweetly and submissively. "I acted the way I thought men wanted me to act," she recalls. "I had a pretty face and a nice body, and men liked that. They also liked me to be sweet, naive, vulnerable, emotional, sort of a victim of others." Those "others" were usually other women. Penny became skillful in making men see her as the sweet, innocent victim of other women. She had learned to play the game with her parents. Penny had blamed her mother for her father's drinking and tried to take her mother's place in her father's affections. As an adult, she saw all women as competitors for the love of all men.

"I never had close girlfriends. Men always seemed to support me whenever I had problems with other women. They'd say things like, 'They're just jealous.' It seemed to be the way things were—the way the whole world was, not the way I was."

Penny's need for male approval became her life's focus. "Nothing mattered to me more than men's approval and affection. I couldn't stand the thought of being without a boyfriend or husband. I always turned to other men with my sad story when things went wrong in a relationship. There were always men I could get to feel sorry for me; I didn't even care if they were married or had girlfriends. I thought that was just the game of life and everyone was playing it, so I had to play to win."

Penny had difficulty seeing the harm she did by lying, manipulating, and scheming behind people's backs. She was convinced she was faultless even with a trail of unhappy relationships and angry, hurt people behind her. "I never thought of myself as having the power to hurt someone else," Penny remembers. "I never thought the things I did and said could have that much effect on other people. I never thought of myself as being mean or harmful to anyone else. I just thought I was doing what I had to do to survive."

When Penny's marriage ended, she began to examine the things she had done to try to make sure men loved her. She had become pregnant deliberately to force her marriage. She had kept in touch with old boyfriends—writing, calling, and seeing them often, even when it upset her husband and the other women involved. She had convinced herself that her intentions were completely innocent. She had lied and manipulated in many other ways, most of which she had denied to herself.

As she recognized her behaviors, Penny began to understand the child within her who still needed her father's love. "The realization that I had hurt a lot of people was hard to take at first. I had never intended to harm anyone. But the truth was, I had hurt all of us—my parents, my men and women friends, my husband, my son, even myself. I don't blame anyone else anymore. Accepting responsibility for the harm I caused was the only way I could clean the slate and move on. I had to make peace with my past before I could learn to live in the present."

Just as Penny did, we're now facing the truth of how we've hurt other people. And we're beginning to clean the slate of our past and move forward on our spiritual journey.

Preparing to Make Amends

The second part of Step Eight is becoming willing to make amends to those people we've harmed. Again, as in Step Six when we became ready to ask God to remove our character defects, in Step Eight we are willing to make amends but we aren't doing it yet. This Step prepares us to face the persons we've harmed, either face-to-face or in some other way, and to make amends. This preparation involves honesty and thoroughness when we list the people we have harmed. It also calls for humility in our forgiveness of ourselves and others for imperfections and misdeeds, and acceptance of our responsibilities as members of the human community. Step Eight is the beginning of the end of our isolation, and the beginning of learning to live harmoniously with others.

Preparing ourselves for making amends requires looking at each situation and relationship from all sides. This helps us gain a clear, honest perspective. We forgive ourselves and others for whatever our contributions may have been to the harm done. If we've not truly forgiven ourselves and others, old resentments will likely resurface, creating new problems.

When we approach another person to make amends, we concentrate only on our part in the harmful situation or relationship. Becoming willing to make amends to those we've harmed may give us a new perspective on ourselves and others. We need to see ourselves as equal to all other people. Then, we can begin to respect differences between us and others without feeling threatened or becoming judgmental. We begin to recognize the effects of our behavior on others and to take care to harm no one, including ourselves. We learn to love ourselves and others as we are—human, not perfect. We grow emotionally and spiritually and develop real friendships with ourselves and others.

We share this planet with millions upon millions of other people, all imperfect, all searching for their place in the universe. We can fight each other, become isolated from each other, hate each other, accuse and begrudge each other, and make life miserable. Or we can learn to accept each other, forgive each other, help each other, and live together harmoniously, enabling all of us to rise to our full potential. It's not really such a tough choice, is it?

STEP NINE

Made direct amends to such people wherever possible, except when to do so would injure them or others

Each of us knows, when we dare to let our spiritual nature reign, the right act in every case.
Each Day a New Beginning

In Step Eight, we made an effort to become willing to make amends to those we've harmed. Now it's time to turn that willingness into action. This will take much humility and courage, as we face the persons we've harmed, apologize for our wrongs, and try to make amends if we can. It's important to plan carefully how we will do this, and to weigh the possible consequences of our actions. But we shouldn't use careful consideration as an excuse to procrastinate or to avoid carrying out our mission.

Embarrassment and fear may lead us to grasp for excuses to avoid a confrontation with someone we've harmed. But, with our Higher Power's help, we can overcome the fear and embarrassment. By taking Step Nine with honesty and humility, we can make peace with the past. Only then can we move on to living fully in the present.

The persons we've harmed may fall into three categories: (1) persons we now have an important relationship with and need to attend to immediately; (2) persons who will require a more gradual approach; and (3) persons to whom we can never make direct amends.

Generally, persons in the first category are our spouses, children, close friends, and other family members. They've taken the brunt of our character defects most directly and recently. We should attend to these relationships as quickly as possible.

The second category of persons—those who will require a more gradual approach—also need our attention, but not so immediately. These might be our employers, employees, co-workers, friends, neighbors, or other acquaintances. Or they might be people with whom past relationships have cooled, or ones kept apart from us by distance. Amends toward these people may take planning before we approach them.

We'll never be able to make direct amends toward the third category of persons. They either have died or are gone from our lives. Or attempting to make amends would harm them or others.

Now, let's look at each of these categories in greater depth.

True Changes in the Making

The first category probably includes people who instantly came to mind when we started listing persons we had harmed. Our husbands, wives, children, and close friends or relatives may have suffered the most from our destructive behaviors. Having analyzed these behaviors in Step Eight, we're ready to take the actions needed to make amends:

- Face each person and admit the wrong we have done.
- Apologize sincerely.
- Make whatever restitution we can.
- Change our behavior to avoid causing the same harm again.

For example, our need to feel in control may have led us to interfere with our spouse's decisions regarding work or hobbies, or even clothes or hairstyles. We can face our spouse, admit our meddling, and apologize. We can then stop our controlling behaviors and catch ourselves whenever we slip into them again.

In some cases, attempting to undo a wrong may lead us to more controlling behavior. Thus, sometimes it's best to apologize and stop the harmful behavior without trying to rectify a specific wrong. Each situation will need to be analyzed individually and appropriate decisions made regarding the specific amends in each case.

Special care must be taken when dealing with young children. We shouldn't burden a child with confusion and worry by trying to explain feelings and behaviors they're too young to understand. We should not only consider what we need to do for ourselves, but we should be sensitive toward the child's concerns. Even a young child can understand and appreciate a simple, straightforward apology such as, "I'm sorry I haven't been spending much time with you." We can then make direct amends: "Let's spend the whole afternoon together, doing whatever you want to do." We can change our behavior to relate to each other in a healthier, more positive way.

No matter who the other person is, our relief and healing comes not at their or anyone else's expense. How our actions affect others must be considered. And the reactions of others should be respected. While most people will respond to us with compassion and understanding, some may be skeptical or not quite as willing to forgive us as we are to forgive them and ourselves. In these cases, we can only accept their feelings and hope that one day they'll trust our sincerity and accept the changes in us. Humility will help us be considerate of others and avoid new conflicts.

Our experiences with the first category of persons we've harmed may help ready us for the second category—those requiring a more gradual approach. Our concern for others will also be needed for the second category. We should carefully weigh various factors in planning our best course of action for everyone concerned. It may not always be appropriate to jump into an apology or an explanation of what we're trying to do. We can make a sincere effort to reach some people through relaxed conversation; others may require a more structured format. We may need time to let the others know of our ongoing recovery process before facing them with our feelings about our specific behavior. They may need time to observe the changes in us and begin to trust our intentions. In some cases, writing a sincere letter rather than facing a person may be best. But we should be careful not to avoid difficult situations.

Each circumstance will have to be carefully thought out and plans made and implemented for apologizing, making amends, and improving our relationships and behaviors. We can always ask our Higher Power for help. And we can seek help from a spiritual advisor or close friend familiar with the Twelve Step program.

Making Indirect Amends

The third category of persons we've harmed can't be repaid directly for our emotional, spiritual, or material debts. These are persons who are no longer living, who are completely out of our lives, or who would be harmed in some way by our attempt to make amends. In certain cases, some of the persons in the first two categories may fall into this category. Marital infidelity, for example, is not always best rectified by confession. This may cause more harm to an unsuspecting spouse and other people. Even when we discuss infidelity, other persons involved may remain nameless. We can take care to confess only our own, not others' wrongs. We should carefully consider what negative consequences our actions could cause. Remember, we can't gain peace of mind at other's expense.

People who have died or left our lives can only be repaid indirectly, if at all. We can perform a kind action for a deceased person's loved one. Or we can donate time or money to one of the deceased's favorite charities. We should not expect glory or repayment for these acts—they're restitution for our wrongdoings.

We can make similar indirect amends to persons who have moved out of our lives or to whom disclosure of our wrongs would cause more harm. We can write a letter of admission and apology. This letter can then be destroyed. or delivered to our spiritual advisor or a trusted friend who acts as a substitute for the wronged person. This symbolic gesture can satisfy our need to confess and apologize without harming anyone. We've expressed our sincere regret, and wherever possible, made indirect amends.

We shouldn't try to avoid facing others because it may be unpleasant. But to give up some of our defects and to begin healing, we may find it necessary to end or dramatically change certain relationships. For example, we may have to cut off contact with a controlling parent or an alcoholic parent who still drinks. Some day these relationships may heal, but it's possible they never will. We can't change anyone else. Some relationships can't withstand our changes. Some relationships are better left in the past. We have an obligation to do what's best for our recovery process, even if that means ending some relationships.

Again, we may want to write down our thoughts and feelings of forgiveness and sorrow for our part in these relationships, as opposed to seeing the persons involved. Using our best judgment, we may or may not send these letters. The goal here is, without hurting anyone, to make peace with our pasts inside our minds, hearts, and spirits. In many cases, this requires rectifying something we've done, apologizing, and changing our behavior toward someone. Sometimes it's impossible to do all of this.

But we cannot simply apologize for our wrongs, make appropriate amends, and then proceed to live life the same as always. Positive change is an important part of the amends we make. Apologies without effective changes are just more empty promises. Taking care of our minds, bodies, and spiritual growth affects others around us in positive ways. When we treat people with respect and love, concentrate on doing our best, and stop our harmful behaviors, we have a positive impact on ourselves and others.

Positive change is what the Twelve Step process is all about. Step Nine is about stretching ourselves—putting ourselves out into the world in a new, positive way. We're clearing the way for these changes by putting our past mistakes to rest.

Steven's Story

In Steven's childhood home, emotions ran high. When he got home from school in the afternoons, he never knew if his mother would be in the kitchen baking something wonderful and singing a happy song, or lying down in her bedroom, crying. Or she might be raging at him for blowing a horn or spilling his milk. Steven's father might come home laughing and whistling. Or he might come in slamming doors, stomping around, and shouting with such powerful force that Steven hid in a closet until he stopped.

After college, Steven lived alone until he married a quiet, even-tempered woman. "I couldn't stand big displays of emotion. Claire was always the same—calm, rational, and soft-spoken. That's why I married her," he says.

After Steven's two children were born, the house was noisier with the arguing, whining, laughing, and playing of small children. "Their noise drove me crazy, and the petty little arguments they fussed about were more than I could tolerate." Steven even became irritated by their silliness and joyful chatter. He urged Claire to keep them quiet, to "put her foot down" and "not let them get away with all this nonsense."

When Steven was with the children, they looked at books or played quietly. He met any silliness or noise with a sharp, "Stop that right now!" He squelched whining or crying over disagreements or minor injuries just as firmly. "I wanted to teach them to be calm, rational people. They were very smart little kids, and I wanted to get them interested in books and math and science, not imaginary creatures and pointless silliness. I wanted them to grow up to be reasonable, intelligent, self-controlled adults—not crazy, emotional wrecks, like my parents."

His children learned quickly to stifle their boisterous behavior and feelings. Sometimes they forgot, but they quickly silenced themselves. Over time, they started getting many stomachaches and other illnesses.

"I finally realized something was wrong after a trip to visit Claire's brother and his family," Steven recalls. It was time to go home, and we were packing the car. I noticed the kids huddled together in a corner, and I went over to see what was the matter. My son, who was five then, quickly said that his little sister was feeling sick.

"She had been perfectly fine just before that, so this came as a surprise. I looked at her red little face and asked what was wrong. She just pointed to her throat. I took her to the bathroom and washed her face. I looked into her throat, but it seemed normal, and she didn't feel feverish. But she couldn't seem to speak, and her muscles were stiff and tense. I suddenly realized that what she was pointing to was a 'lump in her throat' — that tight, awful feeling that grips your throat when you fight back a torrent of tears. I had made such a big deal about no fussing or whining when it was time to go that my little girl was a knot of unexpressed sadness over leaving her favorite relatives. She and her brother had learned that it was better to be sick than to be sad or mad or even happy. I hugged her and whispered, 'It's okay to feel bad about leaving.' She didn't say a word, but cried silently as we left."

Steven apologized to Claire for repressing the family's normal emotions. They decided together on a new approach to setting limits on the children's noisy play and expression of sad or angry feelings. They consulted their pediatrician about normal behavior for their children's ages and read books on child development. Steven decided that the best way to make amends to his children was to change himself.

"I decided the best way to raise my kids to be calm, rational adults was for me to be one. I stopped yelling at them for expressing emotions. We started occasionally being a little silly together. I learned to laugh more, to recognize feelings and to talk about them, or to just let them be. Instead of telling them to stop fighting, I tried to understand their growing sense of self-esteem and their feelings of rivalry. I got help with working on my unresolved issues and started my journey toward spiritual peace. Now I'm thankful for my kids. Having them has taught me that emotions don't have to be overwhelming and out of control."

Moving Forward

Clearly, Step Nine takes much careful thought and courageous action. It takes humility and perseverance to make the needed confessions, apologies, and amends. We may suffer, hindering our spiritual growth and recovery, if we delay or avoid making amends where we can and should. We also can cause more harm if we're careless or self-centered in our attempts to make amends. As always, we can receive guidance from our Higher Power in working through this Step. We can strengthen ourselves by reviewing and repeating some or all of the prior Steps. We all slip sometimes and need this continuous review.

Step Nine releases us from our past. We can now move forward unburdened by guilt and self-recriminations. We can now feel better about ourselves and our relations with others. We can increase our self-acceptance, our self-respect, and our self-esteem. We've cleared out the past and become ready to live our new lives—free from old, destructive behaviors. We can concentrate now on living in the present—each day, each moment, thoughtfully, lovingly, harmoniously in the world with God and with other people. Working through the spiritual journey of the Twelve Step program is a positive change in itself. We're already feeling its effects. The old must crumble and be swept aside for the new to be built in its place.

We've now achieved the freedom to move forward. We've called upon our courage, humility, honesty, faith, hope, and love. The Twelve Step process is indeed an act of love—love for ourselves and our fellow human beings. We can help make our world a better, healthier, happier place. And we've already begun to do just that.

STEP TEN

Continued to take personal inventory and when we were wrong promptly admitted it

Magnificent gardens are not beautiful only because the flowers are so pretty—they're beautiful because someone is controlling the weeds.
— *Earnie Larsen*

Having completed Step Nine, performing the difficult task of making amends to those we had harmed, we now feel cleansed. The past is finally and completely behind us. We're starting over now with a clean slate. Our lives feel new, fresh, unblemished. But this doesn't mean that we'll go forward from here to live a life of total perfection. We'll slip again, in some ways, at some times. Our goal in "housecleaning" wasn't to attain perfection of character. It was to clear out past wrongs, guilt, and debts that blocked our progress. The first nine Steps taught us how to take inventory, admit our wrongs, and make restitution with honesty and humility. We can use this process for the rest of our lives.

As with actual housecleaning, we don't clean once and then leave things to pile up and fall apart. It's a continual process — picking up, dusting, sweeping, and washing. We regularly do the dishes and put out the trash. And once or twice a year, we go through the whole house for spring cleaning. We maintain our spiritual selves in much the same way. We continually check in to remind ourselves of behaviors and motives to avoid, and to catch ourselves when we slip. Then, once in awhile, we take an in-depth look at ourselves and how we're doing. This self-examination becomes a habit that enhances our lives, keeping us aware of tendencies to slip into self-delusion and destructive behavior. It also keeps us free of accumulating guilt. It prevents our point of view from becoming clouded and helps us develop tolerance of others.

If this introspection sounds like too much trouble, remember that our lives depend on it. We know what it was like before we began this journey of recovery. And we know how far we've come through the Steps we've already worked. We can overcome a temptation to skip over Step Ten by the courage, commitment, and faith we've gained through the previous Steps. There was a time when we never would have believed that we could come this far. We can expect to continue to gain better health and more serenity as long as we focus on maintaining our sanity and continuing our spiritual growth.

Continuing to take a personal inventory can be done in the following three ways: (1) frequent or spot-check reviews, taken throughout the day; (2) one review, taken at the end of each day; and (3) long-term reviews, taken once or twice a year.

Taking these inventories is a good way to be constantly aware of our behaviors and motives. They will help us avoid slipping backward in our recovery process. With honesty, humility, and help from our Higher Power, we can now start on our lifelong process of spiritual growth.

Frequent Reviews

We can make spot-check reviews throughout each day to see if we're slipping into old behavior patterns. This keeps us on top of our actions and motives. Catching ourselves in the act can be an effective way to avoid slipping back. It also keeps us free of guilt as we immediately admit when we're wrong. This keeps mistakes from piling up, possibly leading to denial and further mistakes. Quick, frequent reviews can also help calm stormy emotions before they overtake us.

Throughout the day, we can closely watch our actions, words, and thoughts. We look at the possible outcome of each situation and question our true motives. Can anyone be hurt by this? Are we just making excuses for our defects? Are we acting from the ego or contact with our Higher Power? Are we being honest? If we're feeling angry, resentful, depressed, or afraid, these may be signs that we're slipping back into our old lifestyle.

For example, we may feel depressed sitting behind our desk all day at a job we hate. Maybe the only things keeping us in that job are fears, approval-seeking, or low self-esteem. These painful feelings aren't deserved punishments we must endure; they're signals telling us to make changes.

We must trust our Higher Power enough to let go of our preconceived *shoulds* and allow every part of our lives to take whatever course God chooses. We are, through these Steps, getting better and better at hearing our Higher Power's voice. We can now remind ourselves, several times daily, to listen to and follow that voice. It can be very helpful to review Step Three often—getting back on track means we remain honest and humbly turn our will and our lives over to our Higher Power.

Day's End Reviews

At the end of each day, preferably right before bedtime, we can take a few minutes to review the day's events. We take inventory of our actions, words, and motives. This is a mini-version of our Fourth Step Inventory—objective and in the present tense — but only covering one day. We can watch our progress and see the things we're doing well or at least better. We can review problems carefully, examining our behavior and motives in greater depth than we could, perhaps, in our spot-check reviews. We can catch things and plan action for the next day (or as soon as possible) to right the wrongs. We can gain a valuable perspective on our daily behavior and make needed changes.

A day's end review is an objective observation. What did we do today? With whom did we interact? What did we handle well? What could we have handled better? How? Did we slip in any specific way? Did old behaviors or character traits show up in things we did? What could we have done or said instead? How can we rectify the situation? What have we learned today? How can we use what we've learned? We can remember to avoid excuses and self-righteousness, and focus only on *our* behavior in each situation.

Day's end reviews are important because they remind us to live our lives one day at a time. With the day's events fresh in our minds, we can think about our progress and what needs work. When a movie is made in Hollywood, the director, producers, actors, actresses, and others often gather after the day's shooting to view the "dailies"—the film shot that day. They can then see what worked well and what needs to be rewritten or reshot. Our day's end reviews can be like viewing the "dailies," in that we watch a mental movie of our lives, one day at a time.

Many people find that keeping a journal or diary helps them sort out their feelings, beliefs, and motives to gain a better perspective. A journal can also be useful to refer to when we do a long-term review. In addition, an honest, humble, nonjudgmental day's end review may be just the thing to help us get a good night's sleep.

Long-term Reviews

Long-term reviews, like spring cleaning, are done once or twice a year. We can spend a day, weekend, or longer alone taking inventory for the time since our last major review. A retreat to the mountains, the woods, or the beach is often a good way to concentrate on such a review. We may wish to seek the help of a spiritual advisor or a Twelve Step group or member. In a long-term review, we can see and appreciate our progress and spiritual growth. It can be a chance for us to thank our Higher Power for the help we needed to come this far.

Our changed behaviors result from deep, inner changes we've allowed to occur through working the Steps. These changes have brought us greater peace and serenity than we might have believed possible, and the external circumstances of our lives have changed accordingly. We learned that there is nothing life can send our way that, with our Higher Power's help, we can't handle.

The reason we do a long-term inventory is to observe our progress. We may discover a need to review and rework some or all of the Twelve Steps. We can analyze our actions and motives to uncover problem areas in our lives. We may find destructive behavior patterns and defective character traits resurfacing as well as new ones developing. Once again, we focus only on our part in the situations. We aren't victims of circumstances or other people. Difficult situations can be viewed as opportunities for growth, particularly when we didn't create them ourselves by interfering with our Higher Power's will for us.

With help from our journals or previous written inventories, we can ask ourselves these long-term review questions: How have we been handling a previously troublesome relationship? Is the relationship better, worse, or the same? Have we taken back control of any areas of our lives? Have we slipped back into patterns of caretaking or approval-seeking? Have we been feeling anger, depression, fears, or have we shut down our feelings again? We can ask many more questions and, if we need it, may seek help from our spiritual advisor or a close friend.

Also, let's remember to examine our strengths: Have we shown kindness toward others? Have we remembered to spend energy on our spiritual growth? Have we had patience and tolerance for others and ourselves? Have we grown to trust in our Higher Power's will for us? Have we incorporated honesty and humility into ourselves and our lives? Are we growing, little by little, each day?

Long-term reviews are like regularly working Steps Four, Eight, and Nine over and over again. Once or twice a year we take a good, hard look at ourselves and our lives. We note our progress, identify our weaknesses, make amends, and renew our commitment to continued spiritual growth. These reviews are very helpful in gaining perspective and maintaining our lifelong process of spiritual growth.

But long-term reviews alone aren't enough. We need to take daily inventories to keep us mindful of our ongoing growth. We may be tempted to leave this energetic soul-searching for an infrequent, long-term review—to sweep the dirt under the rug until spring cleaning. But we know now that procrastinating only makes matters worse and impedes our growth.

The three kinds of reviews—spot-check, day's end, and long-term—complement each other and create a structure for continuous self-examination. This self-examination is a cornerstone of maintaining sanity and spiritual growth. Constant adjustments are needed as we progress, one day at a time, through our lives. None of us is ever a completely "finished" person. We can continue to learn and grow every moment of each day. We can stay in touch with our Higher Power and continue developing that relationship forever.

Karen's Story

"I've always been very proud of my high standards," admits Karen, an adult child. "I work very hard at everything I do, not just to do a good job but a great one. Once I had learned to see the negative effects of my perfectionism, I had to stay on guard for it in every area of my life. I learned the difference between my over-inflated idea of good and the realities of good enough."

Karen uses the review process every day. "It's really just a habit of asking myself whether my expectations are realistic, whether my goals are reachable and truly desirable, and whether I'm allowing myself to recognize and enjoy my accomplishments.

"I also try to remember not to inflict my perfectionism on other people, expecting too much of them. I ask myself if I'm accepting 'good enough' achievements of myself and others, or expecting nothing less than super, amazing, wonderful, spectacular ones. It's like a series of 'clicks' that go off in my head throughout the day— little warning bells that let me know I've done something that needs to be attended to before it slips away into the past.

"Maybe it sounds like a lot of trouble—all these questions I ask myself," Karen says. "But it really makes everything so much easier. I think of it as cleaning up as I go along, instead of letting a big mess pile up behind me."

When Karen's questioning turns up an error in a decision or behavior, she can admit it and rectify it immediately. "I never knew how easy it could be to just say, 'I was wrong.' It doesn't cause the end of the world, and I'm not any less because of it, in my eyes or anyone else's. People respect me for it. We all know what it's like to be around someone who can never admit a mistake. It's so much easier to admit it, apologize, then drop it. I've found that no one attacks me when I'm not immediately jumping to the defensive.

"It's helped me get along better with everyone, including myself. I don't drag around a load of old guilt and self-recrimination anymore. I make mistakes, and so does everyone else. That's reality. I can live with it because I deal with my mistakes and then let them go. They aren't still there in the back of my mind, haunting me."

Karen says by keeping track of her tendency to slip into perfectionism, she has gained a new ability to enjoy her real successes. "When I was always worried about not being 'good,' I never saw all the 'good enough' achievements and victories I could have been celebrating. Now I don't miss out on that part of my life."

Taking a Look at Ourselves

Developing the habit of self-examination and promptly admitting when we're wrong has clearly positive effects in our lives. Being aware of our part in disputes can only improve our relationships. Remaining on guard for slips into destructive behavior can improve our lives and help us to keep growing spiritually. We can be free of the guilt of an accumulating list of wrongs. And our fear of being ourselves can vanish as we get used to honesty and humility in our everyday lives. We may also see other people become less defensive and more agreeable toward us.

We can start now to put self-examination into practice in our daily lives. Soon it will become a habit for us, as it did for Karen, and we'll no longer have to make ourselves do it. We see now that we aren't just moving through a process of Twelve Steps after which we are finished or cured. We're developing new ways of living that will reshape the rest of our lives.

The Twelve Step program becomes a part of us. It's there for us to use and reuse whenever we feel the need. We may need to return to it occasionally, or often, to review Steps and strengthen our behaviors and attitudes. In other ways, as with these inventories, we can use the Twelve Steps every day of our lives.

STEP ELEVEN

Sought through prayer and meditation to improve our conscious contact with God *as we understood Him,* praying only for knowledge of His will for us and the power to carry that out

If you are too busy to pray, you are too busy.

Night Light

By now we may have had many spiritual experiences through working these Steps. These experiences have built upon each other to create in us a spiritual awakening. After coming to believe in a Power greater than ourselves, we have come to know God in ourselves and our lives. Our conscious contact with our Higher Power—in turning over our will and our lives to the care of God, admitting our wrongs, and asking for our defects to be removed—has grown into a true knowledge of God's presence in our lives. We now seek to strengthen and deepen this connection through prayer and meditation.

We may be confused about prayer and meditation. We may have been taught, in our religious upbringings, to pray in a specific way at specific times. This rote prayer method may have become meaningless to us as we grew confused about God's and religion's roles in our lives.

Meditation, meanwhile, may be foreign to some of us. Thus, we may be frightened by meditation, which is unfamiliar to us, or turned off by prayer, which is too familiar to us in a negative way. As we've already done in other Steps, we may have to clear out some of our old beliefs before we can understand and accept prayer and meditation into our lives. Those of us who once thought of God as an angry, judging entity, now view our Higher Power as loving and accepting. We can change our negative beliefs about prayer and meditation in the same way.

Prayer and meditation are two parts of the same process—the process of communicating with our Higher Power. We can think of this in terms of a telephone conversation. Prayer is the active part of the process, and meditation is the receptive part. The purpose of prayer and meditation is to set up and maintain an open channel of communication between our conscious minds and God.

As we've learned, there's much in our conscious minds to obstruct our reception of our Higher Power's voice—old negative tapes, fears, and doubts. This is why we need meditation—to clear the line. A telephone through which we can speak, but not hear the other voice, isn't much good. It's often equally difficult for us to know what things to pray for to improve our lives. This is why Step Eleven suggests praying only for the knowledge of God's will for us and the power to carry it out.

Here again, as throughout the Twelve Steps, we're trying to get our self-will out of the way so our Higher Power's will can take over. We're all connected to God, wishing to be good, kind, and loving. Nevertheless, we might have impeded our ability to channel God's positive energy into the world. Prayer and meditation help us establish and maintain contact with our Higher Power, allowing peace, love, and serenity to flow into us and through us to others. Here, peace means a lack of conflict with others; serenity means inner tranquility. Prayer and meditation help bring God's will into our conscious minds.

Prayer

In prayer, we actively thank God for the miracles in our lives and ask for the help we need. We may be used to asking for material things or specific events in prayer. But we've learned that we don't often know what's really best for us, and therefore, what to ask for.

Step Eleven suggests that the best way to seek our Higher Power's help is by asking for guidance—knowledge of our Higher Power's will for us. We ask that our will be changed to reflect God's will.

We ask for our defects, fears, and doubts to be removed. We can also ask our Higher Power what we should do about certain people or situations. We ask for help in accepting whatever our Higher Power's will brings into our lives or removes from our lives. We thank God for the positive changes in our lives, for our growing consciousness and spirituality.

Prayer—one person talking to God—is one way of growing spiritually. We can use any of the many meaningful prayers others have composed, or we can use our own words. Sincerity and humility—not poetic verse—are the keys to successful praying. Remember, we need no church or religious beliefs to follow the Twelve Step program. Prayer is a personal activity.

Libraries have many books of prayers composed throughout the ages. These prayers can be poems, songs, and essays. We may find certain prayers that inspire us to improve our outlook and, consequently, our behavior. We may find certain prayers to be helpful in specific instances. The Serenity Prayer, for instance, is often helpful in its brevity and its all-encompassing message:

God grant me the serenity
To accept the things I cannot change,
The courage to change the things I can,
And the wisdom to know the difference.

We can say this prayer frequently throughout the day, any time, any place. It's appropriate for nearly any situation.

Prayers can take many forms. We can read them, sing them, make them up, or write them down. Praying can take an hour or an instant. We can communicate between ourselves and our Higher Power in whatever way feels right to us. Praying first thing in the morning and reading inspirational daily meditations can help us keep the channel open between ourselves and our Higher Power.

Like our Step Ten inventories, we can pray often, daily, and occasionally for longer, more intense periods of time. Whenever we're doing an inventory is a good time to pray. Many moments throughout the day—when we're waiting for an appointment, driving a car, riding a bus or train, or standing in line—can be ideal times for prayer. Ending our days with prayer can also keep us focused on our conscious contact with God, even as we sleep.

Meditation

There are many forms of meditation but all have one basic purpose—eliminating or reducing mind chatter so we can hear God's voice. We focus on just being, rather than doing anything. We quiet our conscious minds by emptying them of thought. Then we can focus on something simple like darkness or bright light or the number one. The main objective of meditation is complete relaxation and centering the mind and body. Being "centered" means being here now, not worrying about yesterday, tomorrow, or even what may happen ten minutes from now. By focusing on something specific and close to us, like our breathing, we can block distracting thoughts about other places, times, and people.

We can, at least at first, find a quiet space to meditate where we'll not be disturbed. We may want to take the phone off the hook, close the doors, and if others are around, let them know we don't want to be interrupted.

Lying flat on our backs or sitting up with our spine straight, we might want to close our eyes, and then relax, breathing deeply and slowly. We can slowly count backward from ten or focus on some other method of mental relaxation. We can imagine ourselves in a quiet setting—alone on a deserted beach, in a field, in the woods, on a mountaintop. This should be a beautiful, natural place where we feel comfortable and safe. We can visualize being there—alone, quiet, and peaceful. We can close our eyes and return to this place for a few minutes whenever we need to calm down, rest, or renew our contact with our Higher Power.

We need not restrict our meditation to twice daily. Meditation can be done almost anywhere, anytime, for a minute or fifteen or thirty minutes—any amount of time that feels comfortable to us. It can be as easy as taking a few minutes to concentrate on the present moment—just observing our breathing, thinking, and being.

When we first begin meditating, we may find that a minute is as long as we can focus—or unfocus—our minds. That's fine. The more we practice this mental relaxation, the longer we'll be able to do it, and the greater the benefits will be.

At the end of each meditation period, we may want to take a couple of very deep breaths as we gently return to our normal consciousness. We may want to go further in practicing meditation by taking up a discipline such as yoga, tai chi, or transcendental meditation to learn to relax and quiet our conscious minds. But it may not be necessary to do anything more than the simple meditations described in Appendix D.

Opening Prayer Channels

Meditation is different from prayer. In prayer, we thank our Higher Power for blessings in our lives and for our spiritual progress; we ask for help to know God's will for us and to act on it. In meditation, we listen for God's answers to our prayers. By quieting the mind chatter, we are better able to listen for and recognize our Higher Power's will for us.

We don't always receive God's answers during meditation. But meditation helps us to open a channel of communication and recognize the answers when they arrive. We may find the answer to a problem soon after we begin making meditation a habit, or the problem may seem to resolve itself. A new way of looking at a problem may suddenly occur to us, or we may receive the help or advice we need from another person or even a book we read. If we open our channel, God will find a way to tell us what we need to know.

The deep relaxation of meditation benefits both our minds and our bodies. It reduces the stress we carry around with us and calms and relaxes us for the rest of the day. It helps us to remain tranquil when facing difficulties and to let go and let God handle our lives. This same tranquility allows us to hear the voice of our Higher Power, through our intuition or through other, external sources. It quiets the static on our telephone line to God.

Margot's Story

As a working mother, Margot spent her off hours doing household chores, shopping, running errands, and driving her children to and from various activities. In addition, she often helped her children with their homework, sewed costumes for school plays, and volunteered as a Scout leader.

"I was always careful not to let my work interfere with trying to be a good mother," Margot remembers. "But I never thought about what both of those things were taking away from me and things I needed to do for myself." After looking at her life, she was able to give up some of her old caretaking and people-pleasing behaviors. In the process, Margot learned to say "no" and to accept help from others.

"Somebody pointed out to me that I only have 100 percent of myself, and if I spent 50 percent on my work and 50 percent on my family, there wouldn't be anything left. I had to readjust the percentages of time and energy I spent on the things I needed to do."

One thing Margot needed to find time for was her spiritual development. "I started reading inspirational books while I waited for my children in the dentist's office or at music lessons. I started praying in the shower every morning. It's just the right amount of time, and I have privacy and quiet. I developed a form of prayer that I use every day. First, I thank God for all the blessings in my life. Then I ask for my defects to be removed, for my will and my life to be taken over by God, and for my continued spiritual healing and growth. Then I ask for help in the day ahead. It's such a positive way to start my day."

Margot says she also prays while vacuuming, driving, riding in elevators, and cooking. "It's a natural part of my thinking now. It's not something I have to make myself do."

Beginning meditation was more difficult for Margot. "It seemed like a waste of time—sitting quietly alone, emptying my mind of all thoughts. It sounded bizarre and felt strange at first, different from anything I'd ever done. But I tried it anyway." Margot tried meditating at various times throughout the day and finally settled into a schedule that worked best for her.

"Once I had practiced it a few times, I started feeling the physical and mental relaxation and spiritual openness that I had been told to expect from meditation. Now I set my alarm clock a few minutes earlier, so I can meditate every morning before I get out of bed. During the day, I sometimes meditate on my coffee breaks or at lunchtime, especially if I'm feeling particularly tense. I always try to find a few minutes after work and before dinner for quiet time. The children do their homework or read, dinner's in the oven, and I go off by myself to meditate. It's a great help in making the transition from work to home. It relaxes me, centers me, and helps me to focus on the present moment."

Rearranging her schedule to allow for conscious contact with her Higher Power has proven well worth the effort for Margot. "If I can find time for prayer and meditation," she laughs, "anyone can. Once I started, I never wanted to stop. It makes me feel so much better. I have more patience, more confidence, and a more positive attitude. It makes me feel focused, centered, and purposeful, instead of scattered, hassled, and tired. I enjoy my work more, my children more, and myself more. I'm not about to stop now!"

Affirmations

One other kind of communication with our Higher Power isn't really a prayer because it isn't telling or asking God anything. It's not really meditation because it's active rather than receptive and quiet. But it does help to open lines of communication between us and our Higher Power. It's called an *affirmation*. An affirmation is a positive statement that we make to ourselves. It helps us to clear out our old, negative tapes, replacing them with new, positive thoughts.

For example, as adult children, many of us grew up with powerful messages telling us that we were worthless. We can reduce the power of this old message and eventually eliminate it by affirming that we are loved by God, ourselves, and others.

A list of affirmations can be found in Appendix D. Each of us can create affirmations to suit our unique needs. Remember that affirmations should always be positive, short, easy to say, and in the present tense. For example, "I now relax and enjoy life."

Faith in our Higher Power and persistence in practicing prayer, meditation, and affirmations can have astonishing results. We can continue to develop our relationship with God daily through conscious contact. We can allow our Higher Power to change our lives, one day at a time. We can find peace and serenity through an open channel that allows God's positive energy to work in us and through us. We can live the rest of our lives, guided by our Higher Power, in emotional well-being. Our spirits have indeed been awakened— brought forth from a fitful sleep into the glorious light of day.

STEP TWELVE

Having had a spiritual awakening as the result of these steps, we tried to carry this message to others, and to practice these principles in all our affairs

What we practice, we become.
— Earnie Larsen

Here we are at Step Twelve of our Twelve Step program. This is the last stop, the end of the line, the goal we've been aiming for from the start. But it's much more than the end of something. It's the beginning of a new way of life, of a lifelong journey of growing awareness, love, peace, and serenity.

It's only the end of our former, unhappy lives. T. S. Eliot wrote, "The end is where we start from." This new way of life can open us up to all the possibilities of God's universe. We can use the Twelve Steps over and over to resolve specific issues or problems. We can go back and use one or more of the Steps again whenever we feel the need.

Moving through the Steps, we have gained knowledge, and something deeper and more difficult to put into words—a *spiritual awakening.* Along the way, some of us may have renewed our relationship with churches or religions; others of us may never feel comfortable with such things. Fortunately, our spirituality is quite separate from our religious affiliations. It's within each of us, not outside us. We have found, through working these Steps, a knowledge of our spirituality and a relationship with our Higher Power. We now know that we have help, guidance, love, and peace within our reach.

We go forward now, not to lives free of problems, setbacks, and even catastrophes. Nothing has changed, and yet everything has changed—we have changed. We can now view difficulties as opportunities for growth. We can now make decisions with faith that our Higher Power is guiding our every move. Whatever happens, even if it seems difficult, will be for the best. We look now for the lesson in every experience and relationship. We can live in each present moment as it occurs, free of guilt from the past and anxiety over the future.

As children of alcoholic or other dysfunctional families, we may have come to adulthood already burned out. We may have fantasized that once we grew up and moved away from our childhood homes, we would be free of the tension, anxiety, crises, fears, and unhappiness in life. When our adult lives presented us with still more difficulties, we may have responded with outrage, "I already paid my dues! No more!"

The normal trials of adulthood may have overwhelmed us, making us feel cheated of what we saw as our earned right to enjoy a problem-free life. But we've learned through these Steps that the real problem in adulthood is within ourselves.

Handicapped by character defects resulting from our childhood experiences, we tried to cope with adult life's normal challenges. We found ourselves blocked and confused within, causing us difficulties without. Through the Twelve Step process, we've cleared out at least some of our barriers to spiritual freedom and well-being.

Our spiritual awakening didn't come instantly. No lightning bolt struck and suddenly enlightened us. Our spiritual awakening grew gradually, depending on the energy we've invested in our spiritual growth.

Sharing Ourselves with Others

With our new outlook, our new behaviors, and our new relationship with our Higher Power, we can now turn our attention outward; we can share our experiences and insights with others. We don't try to convince or convert people, nor tell them what they should or shouldn't do. We simply share ourselves. We tell them our stories— where we were, what we've been through, and where we are now.

Often, by witnessing our recovery, our new serenity and positive energy, many people will share in our experience and begin their own spiritual journey.

We share our stories because others need to know that it's possible to recover, to heal, and to find peace, serenity, and relief from the effects of growing up in a dysfunctional home. They need to know that others have been through it and succeeded. They need to know that they aren't alone. They need us to mirror for them that part of themselves that will work diligently and patiently toward recovery. They need to begin dealing with other people in a healthy manner, and we're the people best equipped to understand them and their difficulties.

By helping others, we also help ourselves. We need to know the intangible rewards of helping other people—of giving without expecting anything in return. Like love itself, the message of the Twelve Steps is renewed in us when we give it to others.

In sharing our stories, we should remember not to overwhelm people with our zeal. While we may be enthusiastic about the wonderful results we've had, we shouldn't become evangelistic in carrying the message to others. We don't preach, teach, or promote the Twelve Step program. The program attracts people who need it, want it, and are ready for it. We simply share our experiences, our stories with others who need help. It's up to them to choose what to do with the information. We aren't superior to them, and we aren't responsible for their recovery.

We've learned, through these Steps, that we can't change others, nor should we try. We can simply tell our stories and make ourselves available to others—to talk, to listen, to encourage, or to help at Twelve Step meetings. Helping others in this way reminds us to maintain our recovery and spiritual growth.

Because slips will happen, we need reminders to keep up our lifelong growth process. We need to keep our never-ending spiritual growth alive. We need to keep working on issues important to us because of our adult child vulnerabilities. We are particularly vulnerable to chemical dependency and compulsive behaviors, and we need to watch closely to prevent their emergence.

Even if our Higher Power has seemingly removed many of our character defects, we must watch out for their return. Just as recovering alcoholics must renew their resolve to avoid drinking every day of their lives, we too must tend to our weak areas daily. These vulnerabilities don't disappear after we've worked through the Twelve Step process. They're with us for life. But the Twelve Steps can now help us keep these vulnerabilities from controlling our lives.

The Twelve Steps can be used in every area of our lives, for the rest of our lives. The Twelve Step program isn't just a tool for recovery—it's a way of life. It may be tempting, when we're feeling better than we ever have before, to put the Twelve Steps aside and feel finished with them. But we live our lives one day at a time. And without a continuous effort to renew our spiritual growth, the inevitable minor slips can become major setbacks. We haven't worked this hard, nor come this far, just to throw it all away.

David's Story

David, an adult child, had been married for several years before he began therapy and joined a Twelve Step fellowship. His marriage had many ups and downs over the years, and the couple had considered divorce. "I learned in recovery that of the many mistakes I had made in my life my marriage wasn't one of them," David says. "I really wanted it to last and to work for both of us. I knew I had done a lot of damage to our relationship, but after I had worked through the Twelve Steps the first time, we agreed to start over with a clean slate."

Although they were both committed to their relationship, David and his wife still had many problems to work out. Sometimes old patterns crept into their behavior, and they faced new problems as well. "I kept telling myself that if I continued to work on my recovery, things would have to get better between us. If I was better, then it would follow that my relationships would be better too." David reminded himself often to let go of controlling behaviors, to resist blaming others and concentrate on his own behavior, and to pray for help and guidance.

"I didn't become perfect by a long shot," David says. "But when I did slip into a negative behavior, I knew it right away. I wasn't kidding myself anymore. That made a big difference in the contribution I could make to our relationship." Humility is truth. David learned to live with the truth and to use it to help him in his relationship with his wife. With humility, David let God take over his will and his marriage. David didn't stop making mistakes. But he learned to recognize them and admit them immediately.

"Every night I spent a few minutes praying and reviewing the day. Sometimes I could look back and feel great about the way I had behaved and the things that were happening in my marriage. Sometimes I would realize I had messed up in some way. But instead of feeling guilty about it, I'd thank God for showing it to me, talk to my wife about it, and then let it go. If there was some sort of amend to be made, I'd make it right away instead of putting it off. That way, the next night it wouldn't still be there, making me feel bad."

Sometimes, David felt discouraged or impatient with himself or with some persisting behaviors he believed he had grown beyond. But when he took a long-term inventory, he found great improvements in his relationship with his wife.

"After six months, I could really see the changes. We talked instead of arguing or sulking. We did more things together. We enjoyed each other's company more. That old undercurrent of anger and mistrust was gone. We still had problems, but we did something about them instead of pretending they didn't exist."

David's marriage continued to improve as he focused on turning over his will to God and on being open and humble. He followed the Twelve Step path to a happier, healthier marriage.

David had stopped going to his fellowship meetings because he "didn't feel sick anymore." But when a friend refused to go to meetings because he said he didn't want to "sit around listening to a bunch of people who were as bad off as he was," David realized that there was another reason to go: he now felt he had something to give. He persuaded his friend to attend a meeting with him. There, David spoke about his past life, his recovery process, and the improvements in his life. He told the group that if he could do it, they could too. He told them that it would be worth going through everything they had to go through to get better.

"I never used to think I had anything to offer other people," David says. "Now I have the Twelve Steps. They're inside me, a part of me. I use them every day of my life, and I give them away whenever I can. When I see other people growing, changing, healing—it just makes me feel so good! And it reminds me to keep working on my process of becoming better and better every day."

A Healthy, Happy Lifestyle

Our inner growth has profound effects on our outer lives. Many of our relationships may have improved since we began working the Twelve Steps. We may have seen dramatic, positive changes occur, and we feel healthier than before. Even things we seemingly have nothing to do with may improve tremendously. We may seem to have better "luck" now attracting harmonious relationships and beneficial events into our lives. These outward signs reflect our spiritual awakening and our Higher Power's influence in our lives.

We can continue in this positive way of living as long as we care for ourselves and remain open to our Higher Power's help. We've gained, through the Twelve Steps, a spiritual connectedness that will help us cope with problems in a healthy, adult fashion. We can continue to care for ourselves by eliminating unnecessary anxiety from our lives, eating properly, sleeping enough, and exercising regularly. Also important is getting regular medical and dental care, praying and meditating, continuing to take inventories and dealing with our errors promptly, and reading inspiring literature. Other self-care exercises include sharing our stories with other people, accepting help from others, and helping others whenever we can. We can now give ourselves what we need for true well-being. If we remember to put our spiritual growth first, everything else will naturally follow.

We started this journey with the understanding that even positive change can be frightening. We now know it can also be rewarding. The changes we've made through taking the Twelve Steps in spite of our fears have led us to a spiritual awakening. We have begun, through these Steps, to recognize our self-worth. We're all a part of humanity, a part of the universe, a part of God. Our recovery and continued growth contributes to the whole of life.

There's no standing still—there's always movement, either forward or backward. Let's now move forward—fortified and blessed with the Twelve Steps—knowing the permanency of our recovery depends solely on us. We can continue our spiritual development for the rest of our lives, returning to the Twelve Steps again and again as we make our never-ending journey of spiritual evolution. The Twelve Steps will always be here for us, like old friends, to lead us back to love, peace, and serenity.

APPENDIX A

Organizations that Can Help

Al-Anon/Alateen Family Group Headquarters, Inc.
P.O. Box 862 Midtown Station
New York, NY 10018-0862

Adult Children of Alcoholics
Central Service Board
P.O. Box 3216
Torrance, CA 90505

Alcoholics Anonymous World Services, Inc.
P.O. Box 459 Grand Central Station
New York, NY 10163

Children of Alcoholics Foundation, Inc.
200 Park Avenue
New York, NY 10166

National Association for Children of Alcoholics
31582 Coast Highway, Suite B
South Laguna, CA 92677

National Clearinghouse for Alcohol and Drug Information
P.O. Box 2345
Rockville, MD 20852

National Council on Alcoholism
12 West 21st Street
New York, NY 10010

APPENDIX B
Suggested Reading

Beattie, Melodie. *Codependent No More*. San Francisco: Harper/Hazelden, 1987.

Black, Claudia. *It Will Never Happen to Me*. Denver: MAC Publications, 1982.

Dean, Amy E. *Once Upon a Time: Stories of Hope from Adult Children*. San Francisco: Harper/Hazelden, 1988.

Dean, Amy E. *Making Changes: How Adult Children Can Have Healthier, Happier Relationships*. Center City, Minn.: Hazelden Educational Materials, 1988.

Gravitz, Herbert L. and Julie D. Bowden. *Recovery: A Guide for Adult Children of Alcoholics*. New York: Simon & Schuster, 1985.

Halpern, Howard M. *Cutting Loose: An Adult Guide to Coming to Terms With Your Parents*. New York: Simon & Schuster, 1977.

Hirschfield, Jerry. *My Ego, My Higher Power, and I*. Farmingdale, N.Y.: Coleman Publishing, 1985.

Klaas, Joe. *The 12 Steps to Happiness*. Center City, Minn.: Hazelden Educational Materials, 1982.

LeShan, Lawrence. *How to Meditate: A Guide to Self-Discovery*. Boston: Little, Brown, & Co., 1975.

Lindquist, Marie. *Holding Back: Why We Hide the Truth About Ourselves*. San Francisco: Harper/Hazelden, 1988.

McConnell, Patty. *Adult Children of Alcoholics: A Workbook for Healing*. San Francisco: Harper & Row, 1986.

Missildine, W. Hugh. *Your Inner Child of the Past*. New York: Simon & Schuster, 1982.

Peck, M. Scott. *The Road Less Traveled: A New Psychology of Love, Traditional Values and Spiritual Growth*. New York: Simon & Schuster, 1978.

Schaef, Anne Wilson. *Co-dependence: Misunderstood—Mistreated.* Minneapolis: Winston, 1986.

Seixas, Judith S. and Geraldine Youcha. *Children of Alcoholics: A Survivor's Manual.* New York: Harper & Row, 1986.

Woititz, Janet G. *Adult Children of Alcoholics.* Hollywood, Fla.: Health Communications, 1983.

Woititz, Janet G. *Struggle for Intimacy.* Hollywood, Fla.: Health Communications, 1985.

The following meditation books in the Harper/Hazelden Meditation Series are also recommended:

Days of Healing, Days of Joy (for adult children), by Earnie Larsen and Carol Larsen Hegarty

Each Day a New Beginning (for women)

Touchstones (for men)

The Promise of a New Day, by Karen Casey and Martha Vanceburg

Night Light, by Amy E. Dean

The Love Book, by Karen Casey (illustrations by David Spohn)

Today's Gift

APPENDIX C

THE TWELVE STEPS OF
ALCOHOLICS ANONYMOUS*

1. We admitted we were powerless over alcohol—that our lives had become unmanageable.

2. Came to believe that a Power greater than ourselves could restore us to sanity.

3. Made a decision to turn our will and our lives over to the care of God *as we understood Him.*

4. Made a searching and fearless moral inventory of ourselves.

5. Admitted to God, to ourselves, and to another human being the exact nature of our wrongs.

6. Were entirely ready to have God remove all these defects of character.

7. Humbly asked Him to remove our shortcomings.

8. Made a list of all persons we had harmed, and became willing to make amends to them all.

9. Made direct amends to such people wherever possible, except when to do so would injure them or others.

10. Continued to take personal inventory and when we were wrong promptly admitted it.

11. Sought through prayer and meditation to improve our conscious contact with God *as we understood Him,* praying only for knowledge of His will for us and the power to carry that out.

12. Having had a spiritual awakening as the result of these steps, we tried to carry this message to alcoholics, and to practice these principles in all our affairs.

---

*The Twelve Steps are taken from *Alcoholics Anonymous* (Third Edition), published by A.A. World Services Inc., New York, N.Y., pp. 59-60. Reprinted with permission.

APPENDIX D

Meditations

What follows are five suggested ways of meditating.

Meditation One

Sit comfortably in a chair or cross-legged on the floor with your back straight. Relax, close your eyes, and breathe deeply and slowly. Focus your attention on your breath—coming in, going out, coming in, going out. As you inhale, silently count slowly to five, and as you exhale, count slowly to eight. Concentrate on your counting and breathing. When your mind wanders into other thoughts, gently return it to your breathing. Just watch your breath flowing into your nostrils and out of your mouth. Do this for as long as you feel comfortable and can keep your attention focused on your breathing.

Meditation Two

Sit or lie down comfortably with your back straight. Relax, close your eyes, and breathe deeply and slowly in a relaxed, natural way. In your mind, count slowly down from ten, relaxing your muscles beginning with your feet and moving up to the top of your head with each count. When you have counted down to one and your body is completely relaxed, let your thoughts drift. Feel how very relaxed you are. Allow yourself to sink into this relaxed feeling. Let your thoughts drift lightly and don't grasp onto any idea or engage in any mental discussion. If your mind tends to do that, observe that it is happening and then let it go. Remain quietly alert, but not holding onto any particular thoughts. Be calm and relaxed for a few minutes. Don't think about the past or the future. Feel where you are now.

Meditation Three

Sit or lie down comfortably with your back straight. Relax, close your eyes, and breathe deeply and slowly. Focus your attention on your breathing. As you exhale, imagine that you are releasing all your tension, anxiety, anger, fear, resentment, frustration, worry, self-hatred, self-pity . . . everything you don't want to have within you. If you like, you can picture this as grey clouds flowing out of you as you breathe. As you inhale, see yourself taking in hope, love, joy, relaxation, serenity, confidence, faith, energy, vitality, health, strength, or any quality you want to have more of for your well-being. If you wish, you can see this as bright white light entering your body with every breath. Keep feeling these qualities flowing into you with each breath, and all the negative feelings flowing out of you as you exhale.

Meditation Four

Sit or lie down comfortably with your back straight. Relax, close your eyes, and breathe deeply and slowly. Concentrate your attention on your breathing until you feel deeply relaxed, Now focus your thoughts on a particular feeling or quality you would like to have more of in your life—serenity, peacefulness, acceptance, under-standing, forgiveness, health, strength, or any positive energy you wish to have for your well-being. Feel that particular energy filling you up. Stay with the feeling for as long as you like, gently bringing your thoughts back to the quality whenever your mind wanders or thinks too hard. Keep the feeling of the quality as long as you can without analyzing, debating, and trying too hard to think about it—just feel it.

Meditation Five

Sit or lie down comfortably with your back straight. Relax, close your eyes, and breathe deeply and slowly. Focus your attention on your breathing and relax your body. When you feel completely re-laxed, begin to imagine a river or stream flowing clearly in one direction. This is a pleasant, beautiful scene. Now imagine yourself, completely relaxed, floating in the water, letting the flow of the river take you where it will. You are completely safe and comfortable. If you wish, you can imagine the hands of your Higher Power holding you gently on top of the water, guiding you and keeping you safe, or you can see yourself in a raft or on a tube. You are deeply relaxed and unafraid. You are being led through beautiful, natural scenery in the cool, refreshing water. Imagine this as if it is really happening. Just let go and allow yourself to go with the flow of the river, knowing you are completely safe. You aren't trying to control or hang onto anything. You feel completely free and relaxed in the flow of the river.

Affirmations

Affirmations, or positive statements, can be made anytime, anyplace. It's especially good to say affirmations silently to yourself at the end of each meditation session, when you're in a deeply relaxed state. It's best to choose a small number of affirmations to work with at one time, perhaps even just one. Repeating the affirmation over and over, you will fill your mind with the positive idea and feeling, replacing your old, negative tapes. If you repeat affirmations in a relaxed, meditative state, you're reaching even deeper into yourself to change your old thoughts and beliefs. It may be helpful to make tape recordings of yourself saying the affirmations over and over to listen to whenever you can.

The following are some affirmations that may be appropriate for many adult children. Choose only those that are meaningful for you, and feel free to make up your own. Remember to make them positive, brief, and in the present tense. For example, if you're working on having a specific behavior removed, instead of saying, "I don't _____ anymore," affirm the positive behavior you want to replace it, or affirm that your Higher Power is now removing the behavior or underlying trait. As you say the affirmations, try to suspend your doubts, and for the moment, truly believe the affirmations.

- I always hear the voice of my Higher Power clearly and accurately and act on it appropriately.
- Every day I am getting better and better.
- I am now attracting healthy, loving relationships into my life.
- The light and love of God are now working in me and through me.
- I now let go of all my barriers, fears, and doubts.
- I now forgive everyone in my life.
- I am an open channel of universal love.
- The world is a wonderful place to be.

- I love and care for myself.
- I forgive myself for all my past mistakes.
- I now relax and enjoy life.
- I am always relaxed and centered.
- I am now following the will of my Higher Power in all things.
- I am now guided by my Higher Power in everything I do.
- I accept and own all of my feelings.
- I now enjoy deep inner peace and serenity.
- God is with me, whatever I'm doing.
- I am now ready to accept happiness into my life.
- I am healthy and full of energy.
- I love other people who love and care for themselves.
- I can now relax and let go.
- I can go with the flow of life.
- My Higher Power is always taking care of me.
- Everything that happens can be for my highest good.
- I now look for the lesson in everything.
- I feel confident and comfortable with other people.
- I am now living in harmony with the divine plan of my life.
- I live one day at a time, with God's help.
- I feel healthy and I love myself.
- I now dissolve and release all the barriers within me.
- My past is finished and I am free of it.
- Love flows freely through me.
- I now follow my Higher Power's will for my highest good.
- I deserve to be happy, and I am.
- I love my body, my mind, and my feelings.
- I am now focused on my Higher Power's will for me.
- I can now give and receive love freely.
- I am open to the voice of my Higher Power.
- I am relaxed and accepting of God's will for me.

INDEX